# Personal Impact

MICHAEL SHEA

# Personal Impact

*Presence, Paralanguage*
*and the Art of Good Communication*

LONDON   NEW YORK   SYDNEY   TORONTO

This edition Published in 1993
by BCA, by arrangement with Sinclair-Stevenson
an imprint of Reed Consumer Books Ltd

Copyright © 1993 by Michael Shea

CN 1707

Typeset by Hewer Text Composition Services, Edinburgh
Printed and bound in Great Britain
by Clays Ltd, St. Ives plc

*Everyone sees what you appear to be: few experience what you really are.*

Machiavelli

*It is sometimes a bit of a shock to be reminded that, in operational and practical fact, the medium is the message.*

Marshal McLuhan

*Most speakers feel that fifty per-cent is what you deliver and fifty per-cent how you deliver it. Masters and Johnson feel the same way.*

Robert Orben

# Contents

# Preface

Psychologists spend a great deal of time investigating how people communicate with one another. This book blends some of their theory with the practical results I myself have encountered while teaching self-projection, public speaking, interview, and other communications skills, to a wide range of people from all walks of life. In part the contents are based on classes and seminars given by me as Visiting Professor of Personal and Corporate Communications at Strathclyde University's Graduate Business School, and to other interested groups, both large and small. They should have general appeal to anyone in business or professional life who have, publicly, to project themselves and their ideas. This is not a 'how to' book, however, since those skills covered, such as public speaking, can only be improved through practice. But it does provide a reference chart which may be useful in developing your overall personal impact.

The book will be particularly helpful to those who are not yet in positions of authority but who wish to advance their careers through making a better personal impact on superiors and those others who might feel inclined to select or promote them. It is a book of guidelines: there is no substitute for having direct personal tuition in impact communication and interview skills from someone who is properly experienced in the art of developing people's ability to present themselves to best effect.

There are many quotations in this book. I have no qualms about being a burglar of other people's words, since they benefit from further recognition and display. These quotes reflect the fact that men and women across the ages have always recognised the importance of communicating in public, and of personal impact skills generally.

# INTRODUCTION

*First impressions are the most lasting.*

Proverb

---

*People will have to take me as I am. The image-makers will not find me under their tutelage.*

John Major on first becoming
Prime Minister in 1990

---

*I'm just waiting for one of you to come up with a robot that can give a public speech. I'm sure it will make my life easier and also yours.*

ex-President George Bush,
to scientists in Albuquerque,
New Mexico

---

As Chairman of a head-hunting company, I know from experience that if three equally well-qualified candidates present themselves for a top job, the successful one will, generally, be the one who communicates best. Good CVs matter, experience matters, but good personal impact not only allows you to stand out but also to rise above your colleagues. 'It is not what you say but how you say it' may be a common enough phrase, but for lots of surprising reasons its message is seldom put into daily practice. While we know deep down within ourselves that it is true, our overall presence and body language and the way we say things, the whole tenor and authority of our voice, gets ignored at the expense of our agonising over the precise words that we intend using. We practise, we spend days writing out the words of our speech or what we are going to say at the interview. We spend little or no time on working out *how* we will say it.

Communicating is like acting. Any audience – from an interviewer sitting at the other side of an office table, to a thousand people in a great conference hall – has to be inspired to listen, and not by your words alone. The overall personal impact made by you, if you want them to listen, is crucial. The perception they have of you is the reality until it is changed. Psychological research has proved conclusively that in inter-personal communication, the visual impression made by you – that is your presence, along with the sound, tone and authority of your voice, what is known as your *paralanguage* – has a vastly greater effect on others than the actual words you use. This package of impressions is given various names, such as rapport, authority, likeability, magnetism, attractiveness, competence, flair, radiance, charisma, the halo effect, or personal chemistry. We are all aware of it and its importance in others, but we pay little attention to developing it in ourselves. This book is about the importance of such impact factors, and how you can easily improve them for more effective inter-personal relations.

Most of us communicate reasonably well in day to day conversation. We get by. But there are other skills needed if we want to increase our prospects and standing to a wider, or a more selective and demanding audience. To take some examples from politics – and I do so occasionally through-out the book because politicians, in terms of projecting themselves, are familiar via the television screens to most people from other walks of life – it is interesting to reflect on the impact and impression made on their fellow men and women by great figures of the twentieth century, such as Churchill, Roosevelt and De Gaulle. We realise imme-diately that it was not so much the words they used – though Churchill's words were undoubtedly impressive – so much as the overall amalgam of authority, of voice, timing, presence and decisiveness – the aura of power that produced the image and made people listen. Denis Healey once remarked, with typical percipience, that Mar-garet Thatcher had 'no hinterland'. One sees what he meant, but she got over it by the way she presented herself in public: a majority listened; while of Neil Kin-nock, the leader of the Opposition for eleven years, it was said that while he had great powers of speech he had none of communication. His verbal tide broke over us, yet little was taken in.

To illustrate the value of some of these skills without always referring to people in the public domain where our political attitudes may occasionally throw us off impartial balance, let me introduce three characters in search of a job, promotion, or seeking to project themselves and some cause which they want others to be persuaded to adopt. These three individuals can come from any walk of life, but let us for the purposes of this exercise assume that they are three professionals in their early thirties whose feet are already on the bottom rungs of the ladder of success.

Our first candidate for preferment is John Hustle who is brash, pushy and glib. So far in life he has passed his professional exams and other career hurdles with relative ease. He is clever and snappy and he knows it. He has the gift of the gab and obviously lost his modesty a long time ago. He has the carpet salesman's answer to everything, smirking his way through his daily responsibilities, and he certainly makes a strong first impression, though not altogether a positive one.

Our second candidate in search of personal success and career advancement is Alan Grey, equally clever, equally well qualified, but who believes that his intrinsic qualities should somehow emerge and speak for themselves. He is a quiet, thoughtful man who places more pauses than words in any statement. His paper qualifications lead him to suppose he will reach the top, but his quiet demeanour, somewhat scruffy dress and deliberate unobtrusiveness, will lead him, if he is not careful, to all the background jobs of life. He seldom smiles unless he knows people: he leaves little or nothing by way of a first impression.

The third candidate for advancement up the career pyramid is David Wright – again a peer, a precise match on paper with the other two in terms of his professional skills and qualifications. But Mr Wright projects a maturer and more positive first impression. He is quietly confident, he smiles agreeably, and consequently appears, on the face of it, to be the likely winner in any direct competition for preferment. But there are pitfalls and problems in store for him as well, and things he will have to learn to improve on just as much as Mr Hustle will have to moderate his brashness and Mr Grey must smarten up in order to get noticed at all. These three individuals, like most of us if we have ambition, will have to present themselves and their ideas in public at some time in their lives. This may be at a black-tie dinner, at a small gathering of friends, at a major public event or at an office party. It may be at a board meeting or seminar, at an Annual General Meeting, in front of the television cameras, or, because they are for whatever reason the focus of brief media attention, with a radio microphone suddenly thrust in front of them. It is absurd if they, like so many of us, prove bad at communicating, ruin good material, and their reputations, by hesitant or leaden delivery and by getting their timing all wrong.

As children, we mostly learn to speak and be understood around the age of three or four, long before we are able to read and write. Seldom are the majority of us given much further clear instruction in later life on how to ennunciate clearly, to communicate in the best possible ways with one another, let alone how to recognise and build up our good presentational points and negate our worse 'flip side'. Even those of us who are fluent in that our words flow out, have to ask ourselves whether we convey an adequate, impressive or effective message. In normal conversation, we speak on average seven times faster than we write. In speeches, as we will see later, we tend to speak slightly slower depending on the size of the audience we are addressing. We benefit from an innate process that quickly marshalls our thoughts and words in an orderly manner before we subject others to them. These words may make sense, but surely we should allocate proportionately more time during our lives to improving how they emerge, as part of our personal communications package?

Because we put so little time into trying to improve, many of us go through life hating or fearing having to communicate in public and as a result we suffer socially and in our working careers. With colleagues, in particular, we adopt a take-it-or-leave-it attitude. We don't try. We make little effort to see ourselves more clearly. Yet the higher up the business or social ladder we get, the more important our image, our ability to speak or be interviewed credibly and well, becomes. We live in a media democracy where, as we move to the top of our chosen career, our personal reputation and the image of the organisation or company we lead or are meant to project matters as much, if not more, than how good we are in private. Public communication skills have much in common with the world of show-biz, for as soon as we get up onto any stage, audiences immediately compare us with the best they have seen or listened to. These may include amateurs or professionals, performers from entertainment, from politics and the like. Our audience will make judgements about us without making allowances for our more modest backgrounds. In consequence, while we may never be able to match the best as we strive to get to the top of our particular ladder, we must increasingly try to reduce the comparative gap, or at least positively differentiate ourselves from others of similar background.

A few ill-chosen or ill-delivered words on a public platform or in a TV interview, or a lack of understanding of our audience, can do the greatest damage not only to our personal advancement but also to the body we are representing. Today, even if we are leaders or senior managers, we cannot hand over the entire responsibility for projecting our views to the media or the public to some paid spokesman, and forget about it. In any event, public relations people get it just as wrong, as did the notorious British Rail 'voice' who explained that trains were being delayed because 'it was the wrong sort of snow'. It did not need a train accident to get them a bad press. Business leaders themselves constantly mishandle their public pronouncements, making fools of themselves, their companies and their products, because they fail to rehearse properly, because they believe they can do as they do in the Boardroom and *ad lib* their way through any event. Remember

Gerald Ratner who remarked that one item sold in his shops was 'crap', adding the flat-falling joke that his '99p earrings cost less than a Marks & Spencer prawn sandwich but don't last as long'. How much did Mr Ratner (who later left the company) and his company have to spend on subsequent public relations to put that one right, to stop his share price plummeting further than it did?

Poor communication and bad personal impact skills are particularly dangerous as you enter this high-profile public domain, since the media lies in wait there and takes great delight in sacrificing its erstwhile business, political or social heroes. Newspapers behave rather like those high priests of the past who, as part of their religious process, created victim kings who were carefully chosen, garlanded, feted, given a brief authority, and then ritually slaughtered. A slip in presentation as much as in behaviour by someone in public life is God's gift to the headline writers of the world.

---

*As a vessel is known by the sound, whether it be cracked or not, so men are proved by their speeches whether they be wise or foolish.*

Demosthenes

---

So why do so many of us, who realise deepdown how important it is, communicate so badly yet make such little effort to improve? One reason for this fault or default, particularly in calvinistic, anglo-saxon societies, is the in-built distrust that exists of those who are too quick with words, too outspoken, too verbally pushy, too glib, too clever by half, too much like our Mr John Hustle. We are wary of what Americans call 'empty suits', the smile-nice, talk-nice, soft-soap people. The 'gift of the gab' is something we believe should be treated with suspicion or, at least, caution. We tend to think that the facts should somehow emerge and speak for themselves. We prefer quiet reason to talkshow-style prattle. Often rightly so. But there is a middle way.

The words we use and the way we deliver them can not only undervalue us but also distort or disguise our true message. Few of us think it sufficiently important to get round to seeing ourselves as others see us, or we rely on occasional truth games with friends or family – family especially. Sadly, serious complaints or criticism of ourselves from such a source frequently lead more to acrimony than betterment. In any event, to spend too much time on such matters leaves us open to accusations of narcissism, or 'posing', or wanting to act a part, or mere vanity. Through life, unless we are particularly blind, we all gradually do acquire a general awareness of certain failings that we have, but for reasons of self-esteem or mere habit, we ignore or marginalise rather than rectify them. Yet, when given the encouragement so to do, we are horrified to see ourselves on a video screen for the first time or hear the sound of our voice on an audio tape. Even after that experience we tend, unless we get prodded, to resign ourselves to having these speech or self-presentation defects without question. 'I don't have the time,' or 'I can't be bothered with that image-improvement rubbish,' or 'I've got along OK so far, so why change?' are among the commonest reactions.

By contrast, some of us, many of us, have already got over-inflated ideas about our own abilities and about how attractive we are to others. We don't ask ourselves whether our actual skills and attributes live up to our perception of them. We make no serious, conscious attempt to analyse our positive and negative aspects in a rational way even when, for example, we have them pointed out to us in annual appraisal interviews or management reviews. We often react badly to specific criticisms that are made of us (usually blaming the critic) and attempt to improve only on those defects that it suits us to address. We may be blinded by our aims and ambitions, and, in the process, develop vague and unstructured views about how other people react to us, simply because we appear to satisfy them most of the time. We may still get promotion, but not as far or as fast as we should. Yet we *can* all improve, and improve quickly. This is what *PERSONAL IMPACT* is all about.

> *Mistrust first impulses, they are nearly always good.*
>
> Talleyrand

We can learn a great deal by examining how we ourselves react to other people. The most cynical, the most intelligent, the most politically mature of us are no different from the *hoi polloi* when it comes to how speedily (and often inaccurately) we assess our fellow men and women. We may deny it but even the most cautious of us are overwhelmingly persuaded by first impressions. We seldom give people we encounter a second chance. When we see someone for that first time, the initial sound/visual 'Bite' – that is the combination of their looks, their dress, their bearing, and the tenor of their opening remarks – become deeply etched in our minds and affect our attitudes to them. A few words or an appropriate or inappropriate gesture can make all the difference for good or bad. That first view, taken in as brief a period as *fifteen seconds*, is both difficult to dislodge and is often the longest lasting. From previous experience of people who we think are rather like them, we jump to conclusions, we prejudge, we compare; we have a far from open mind about their likely abilities. Such pre-set assumptions are known by psychologists as *implicit personal theories*. To overcome these initial prejudices or prejudgements is a long process. Anything the person concerned does in subsequent sightings has a tendency merely to reinforce that first basic reaction. For example, in the USA, in the 1988 Presidential election, a polled seventy-five per cent of the electorate admitted that they had voted for Bush or Dukakis on the basis of *first gut feeling*, which is much the same thing, and the choice of Al Gore as President Clinton's running mate in 1992 must certainly have been helped by the sort of factors that caused *Fitness Magazine*'s women readers to choose him 'on impulse' above Mel Gibson and Tom Cruise as their ideal Fantasy Man. Yet his political ideas were totally unknown to the overwhelming majority of those questioned.

The majority of us end up having an instinctive 'liking' for certain people like Gorbachev or Winston Churchill or the cowboys in the white hats who ride out of the sunset to save the situation. But we are equally programmed to dislike certain individuals because of the way they are first presented to us. Dukakis was, according to experienced political commentators, 'defined negatively' by the Bush campaign in the 1988 presidential election before Dukakis himself, a man who was not well known nationally, could set his own definition and his own first impact on the wider public. This phenomenon is possible in USA, more so than it could be in western Europe, because of the size of that country, the lack of a national press, and a much less closely defined party structure. The image of politicians in the USA is almost exclusively projected via the television screen, while in the UK and western Europe there are other mechanisms for building the image of a politician for better or for worse. We experience this same phenomenon in everyday life: most of us are instantly predefined in other people's minds because of our backgrounds, our upbringing, our professions, our looks, and so on, before we even get to open our mouths.

One reason for all this is not so much prejudice but that most of us are too busy to suspend judgement for long – about strangers, about colleagues, about politicians, about anyone. We adopt brief (and often erroneous) one-adjective ways of describing individuals: kind, stupid, pretty, ugly, bad-tempered. One word is often all that is allowed to sum up a highly-complex person who possesses a whole range of abilities and defects.

Play a game with yourself and see whether one word as opposed to a complex range of thoughts, comes to mind when you start defining what you have been programmed into thinking of as the characters of figures such as Thatcher, Kinnock, Smith, Major, Bush or Clinton. Each time anyone you know's name is mentioned, not just a politician but a colleague at work, a neighbour or even a friend, I suspect you will find that one solitary word or adjective comes to the forefront of your mind in order to describe them. Of our three candidates for advancement, for example, Hustle, Grey and Wright, will, in turn, be labelled brash, boring and likeable when they are all much much more than just that.

On the public platform and on the television screen and

also in one-to-one interviews, the fifteen second rule, that first short sound/visual impact, is near absolute. Thus, your appearance, facial expression, and opening words (delivered in the accent you grew up with or have developed or have trained to use) have to match the occasion. If you dress like a tramp, if you speak with a lack of clarity or lack of assurance, if you look nervous or sullen or unhappy or bored, unless your reputation has in some way already been established, you will be perceived as just that: an indecisive, ill-spoken, uninspiring tramp.

History is littered with unhelpful judgements about people. Quite often they are very unfair. Take, for example, Michael Foot who led the British Labour Party in the early 1980s. He was always presented – in one word – as shambolic, out of keeping with his role as a credible Opposition leader. Had he been in some other area of activity – he is a considerable author, thinker and book collector – he might well have made a much better impact on the history of the second half of the twentieth century. But all he became known for was as the master of the never ending sentence who would have been much better suited to academia or research than to the political stage. Pick up a newspaper: you will find plenty of other one-word examples of this sort of rush to judgement.

Fifteen seconds is not long to make that crucial first impression. Most audiences don't have an attention span that is much longer than that. This, as television advertisers have always recognised, is why you have to sell or say a lot in the shortest time. You have to be clever and slick and know exactly what you want to project. You have to grab people's attention fast to make your point.

The psychological term for these first impressions that people gain is the *Primacy Effect*. Many studies have shown how great that effect is when we first meet someone: our judgement about them is often made on the basis of similar previous experience, since we tend to categorise or pigeon-hole individuals in as consistent a way as possible. One bearded, leather-jacketed biker will, for example, be categorised with another similarly attired individual, even though they are totally different people in every other way. Our attitude towards someone will change very slowly thereafter. If our meetings subsequently become frequent, or if there is a long gap between encounters, then our *most recent* experience of someone, for better or for worse, what psychologists call the *Recency Effect*, increases in importance.

Not only do the Primacy and Recency Effects apply to attitudes to individuals, they also do so to the *message* that person may be delivering. Here too, Primacy, the first time you hear something, sticks and will only slowly be eroded by more recent messages on a similar subject. That is why, as you will see later, making a clear, immediate impact is a prerequisite to delivering the sort of commanding statement that sticks in the mind. Among our candidates for promotion, David Wright, every time we meet him (ie. both in terms of the primacy and the recency effect) will probably project a consistently pleasant and thoughtful image. Alan Grey, by contrast, will probably become slightly more appreciated the more we get to know him, though both sides will have to work hard at it. By contrast, John Hustle who might just have made a bit of a splash on first impression will become irritating and shallower on closer acquaintance. Hustle's problem is that while he will have appeared to be witty and amusing, and full of bouncy good ideas on first meeting, when time really gets to work, his triteness, and the fact that so many of his ideas are borrowed from others or lack depth for one reason or another, become increasingly apparent.

I am not, of course, arguing that every opinion of others depends on instant image, or on first or second impressions. That would be as open to qualification as the famous remark by Laurence Olivier that 'If you can fake sincerity, you can fake anything.' But the cruel fact to remember is that when you are being interviewed by the media or for career reasons, or are briefly on stage to make a speech, you have little time and only one chance to make your mark. You will fall by the wayside of life if you fail to recognise that one simple fact.

What do you do about it? You train yourself to get that first impact right. I am not advocating that you become like actors and actresses who are taught to be what and whom they are not. They convince us and move us by using many different skills and devices. You should convince not by being devious, but by fielding your best attributes properly.

Richard Burton was born with the ability to read from a telephone book and make it sound like great drama. Politicians may, with great gusto, acquire an ease in advocating policies in which they privately have little faith. Lawyers are trained to argue cases in which they have little belief, and for clients in whom they have no real trust. Indeed, in the States, it is now not uncommon for attorneys to be trained at special drama schools in overt and subliminal techniques for 'selling' their clients to impressionable juries. Whatever the ethics of that, of treating a jury not as an arbiter of justice but as an audience as if at a play, we all are guilty, at some time or another, of 'putting on an act' to get a point across, to a loved one, to a colleague, to a child, to a wider audience. We feign or exaggerate amusement, or sorrow, or admiration, or anger, depending on the occasion. In major and in minor ways, even if we are very honest and natural people, we all occasionally try to become a little closer to what we would wish to be seen to be.

This often unconscious process of acting a part becomes more noticeable when individuals move from one walk of life to another. We get very set in our ways of self-projecting, depending on audience: the tough boss may behave in one way with junior colleagues and totally differently with friends in his local golf club. This happens in professional life as well. I can think of a famous member of the Bar who was transferred from there to high political office, but failed miserably in adjusting his habits to his new environment. He expected his recently-acquired political audience

to listen to his ponderous musings, which – entirely appo-
site to, or tolerated in a court room – were totally out of
place in the hurly burly of Parliament. He spoke, as a
former judge of men, as if everything he said had to be
at least respected if not obeyed, rather like some senior
military figures continue to expect obedience when they
move into less disciplined and less authoritarian roles in
civilian life. But even in less obvious circumstances, we all
are guilty of 'acting out', without due care and attention.

Wherever you are now, turn and look at those around
you for fifteen seconds, then, putting out of your mind
what you know about them, judge whether you are impressed by how they present themselves. Look at their
posture, how they appear, sit, dress, inspire immediate
confidence, and exude sincerity. Are they putting on an
act? Are they pretending to be what they are not? Are you
yourself guilty of stereotyping them because of their sex,
race, age or what they are wearing? All these factors, taken
together, will produce their implicit effect on you and on
others, when they set out to convince, to advocate, to sell,
to persuade. If they look good and sound genuine, they
will do better than an opposition that does not. To mis-
quote the late Lord Mancroft, 'We are all born equal, but
quite a few of us get over it by working up our image.'

Like it or not, and alert as we may try to be, psychologists have a point when they argue that we all are pre-
judiced for or against certain types of people, by no means
just over blatant matters of nationality or of race, but also

by their age and sex, over what part of the country they come from, how personable they look, how clearly they speak, how they stand and how they dress – their whole presentational and delivery style. Precise psychological tests demonstrate that, no matter what the content, we are all much more likely to be convinced if a message is given or delivered with sufficient confidence and authority by someone whom we relate well to, someone who is like us, someone who stands tall and inspires immediate respect.

This book is directed both at those who already do a lot of inter-personal communicating in business and on social occasions, people who know their subject and what they want to say, but also at those who are at the beginning of their careers or in middle management, or on the first rungs of their chosen profession. Many of the latter have a great deal to offer, have already acquired numerous professional qualifications but are in danger of losing out in the rat race of life because they have not given sufficient attention to presenting themselves to best advantage to those who are in positions that could influence their future success. It is a question of building on your existing strengths, and adding confidence, poise and persuasiveness. It is not about simple image-making, but, because the agendas of public life are now largely set by the media and mass communication, it has to be read against that background. I do *not* suggest that there is only one way to achieve this, one set of rules, one style of public speaking or of being interviewed on television. Each person must develop their own performance. Each has their own pace and approach. Making a good personal impact goes beyond merely putting on an act, but is about using your existing qualities and existing skills more effectively.

The bookshops of the world overflow with personal improvement texts of a variety of qualities, many of them highly questionable. No book can ever teach the personal skills required to improve your impact on others, yet the great but simple secret is that they can be improved rapidly, provably and lastingly. You need to hold a mirror to yourself, you need friends, you need a video camera, you need training to ensure that your latent characteristics and abilities are properly recognised, not only by others but by you too. My entire approach to teaching depends on this process: getting people to see themselves as others see them. In public speaking seminars or when I am coaching in interview techniques, the quickest way to success is to play-back what has happened on a television monitor. Seventy-five per cent of what happens thereafter is self-learnt. You see what you do well and what you do badly. With guidance from a professional, even your downside can be modified or turned to good advantage by you yourselves. With this book as a guide, matched with a day's training with a professional tutor, you can dramatically improve your chances. There are few gimmicks: success is provable and the skills, once learnt, rather like riding a bicycle, are never forgotten.

# SECTION ONE

# Image:
# Does it Really Matter?

> *Greatness in the Presidential Chair is largely an illusion of the People.*
>
> *Time*

---

> *The great leaders have always stage-managed their effects.*
>
> De Gaulle

---

> *It ain't whatcha say, it's the way howcha say it.*
>
> Louis Armstrong

---

We are almost always most attracted by people and ideas that take us a little further down the path we are already following. We find it more appealing if these individuals and their persuasions come with the right images, ones that suit or match our own personal style and habits. Looking a little deeper into whether personal impact skills matter, we come to realise that what we see is usually more important than what we hear. Admittedly, in life and in our careers, it is our general competence, our social background, our professional, technical, accounting, legal, administrative, computing skills, or whatever, that count. If we can therefore get on with, convince and manage our immediate family, friends, colleagues and subordinates, what need is there to project a better image to a wider or more transitory audience?

The answer, quite simply, is that few of us really want to leave our ambitions at that level. We want to get the maximum out of ourselves like the pupils at my old school who were exhorted by the motto: *Plus est en vous*: there's more in you. Take Messrs Hustle, Grey and Wright, for example. They have set out in their careers or in their search for executive advancement by recognising that they probably need some help, but are not entirely sure what form that assistance should take. They have heard in various imprecise ways, from self-motivated colleagues, from true or less true friends, from frustrated wives or often extremely direct children, and they have had read out to them from their personal report forms, what are perceived to be their strengths and weaknesses. But even very demanding bosses, in such assessments tend, by and large, to be rather too kindly or circumspect. Those whose task it is to report on others (and sometimes it is done rather well) do not want to offend or to be destructively hurtful; often they will have to continue to work closely with one another in the future, and this leads to inadequate people continuing in jobs where with only a little bit of constructive personal impact work they could easily improve.

Good personal impact training starts with having a once-off, no holds-barred assessment of *how* you say what you say and *how* you work at what you work at, presented to you by an *outside professional*, rather than by an inside manager. This can be of real value not only to you, but also to the organisation for which you work. The outside professional can be much tougher, yet much more instructive and helpful in their assessment without the danger of the individual concerned having to share the same acrimonious office space for years to come. This is because they get the client to see for him or herself what, if anything, is wrong and what can be improved.

There are two fundamental reasons for most of us in trying to better our personal image and impact.

1. *For selfish reasons*
    - To get a job
    - To get noticed: the 'I'm Here-ism' factor
    - To get our ideas recognised
    - To get our agendas accepted
    - To get promotion
    - To get selected over others
    - To have an agreeable life: to get on well with people
    - In sum: for career reasons, since the interview, the judging of people by how they appear, is still the predominant method of personal selection in all walks of life.

2. *For good leadership and management reasons*

A good leader or manager has a number of functions in any organisation large or small. He or she has to act as:

– a change maker
– an articulator of strategy
– someone who shows the way
– someone who encourages others to follow
– someone who measures results
– someone who provides the model

For all these leadership functions to be carried out effectively, good personal communication is the prerequisite of all the above in what is the goldfish bowl of top business and public life.

Those who are concerned with any organisation and its image already know how important the outside perception of that organisation is. While the real value of an issue advocated by an organisation may be strong, the reasons for a change in, say, education policy by the Government of the day, or the reasons why a company is making a thousand workers redundant, will often take second place to *how well the case for it is argued and by whom.* One policy in a company, in a club, in a country, is frequently replaced by another not because of merit, but because of the skill and personality of the advocate. This may sound cynical, but it is true.

I have seen this happen inside one particular organisation for which I worked in the past. The Finance Officer in this company was an outstanding but low-key man with poor communication skills who tended to stumble over his words. The impatient Chairman therefore had a habit of ignoring his particular contribution and going instead for a much more lightweight 'suit' – a Hustle type – who was well-spoken, and could marshal his arguments with great rapidity and conviction. The only problem was that the latter's case was ill-considered and the results were disastrous. Everyone round that boardroom table could see what was happening but no-one did anything to stop it. It echoed a remark by Sir James Goldsmith, who once said something to the effect that the person to fear most in any organisation is the one who is enormously industrious, confident, determined, and wrong. In terms of our three case-study individuals, we will find that John Hustle's half-baked, but glibly expressed ideas will often win out over the more thoughtful, yet perhaps less adventurous proposals projected by David Wright, while quite possibly, the best course of action will be rejected or ignored because it has been self-effacingly suggested, in inaudible and self-deprecating terms, by the lacklustre Alan Grey.

The importance of communicating with skill is widely recognised in the wider public arena which is why everyone, from politicians to pop stars, have image advisers, spin doctors, colour-me-pretty experts, PR consultants, advertising strategists, press spokesmen, media analysts, speech writers and other marketing specialists on their staffs. The Tory Party in the 1992 General Election made

no bones about things: they had a 'Director of Presentation', which is what it is all about. Such people know that
the packaging of individuals, giving them the right
personal ballast, wins where content alone will not.

The holding of some 'office', or lack of it, shows up the
skills of individuals in naked relief. Men and women are
listened to with more attention simply because they hold
important appointments, and rank dresses them large.
Most people, even for example the Ronald Reagans and
the Mrs Thatchers of the world are diminished, made
tawdry, almost comic at times, when they leave centre-
stage. The trappings of power, stripped away, can show
the comparative smallness of the human being beneath,
thus proving Talleyrand's remark that 'nations would be
terrified if they know by what small men they are gov-
erned.' There are some, however, like Lord (David) Owen,
who retain a sheen of power even out of office. His erstwhile colleague, Sir David Steel, complete with a slight
Scottish accent which adds a touch of gravitas, has also
retained a continuing shelf-life and an attention-grabbing
style about him, because he has good personal impact skills
and a tendency to look you straight in the eye. Whether you
are meeting them face to face or watching them on a
television screen, each man projects a feeling that he genu-
inely believes in what he is saying. Both retain authority.

Taken to its extreme, the world of show business and
pop music is filled with examples of those whose images
have been created by huge teams of image merchants and

packagers. One only needs to think of the Madonnas or Michael Jacksons of the world to see how the deliberate projection of a culture of extremes, visually and sexually exploitative, has created a persona far greater than the mere singing talent of the individual concerned could possibly deserve. But perception *is* reality. Many such people only exist when their names appear in the gossip and showbiz columns of the world's press. Without the oxygen of publicity, they disappear. Like most ageing politicians, they fade rapidly away.

We will return to this point later, but it is interesting to note that no matter how good someone is at projecting themselves, their image can be rapidly eroded in the short term if they try to speak or are interviewed when tired, or in some other way are unprepared for a demanding media or public audience. Winston Churchill was once asked what he most feared. 'Events,' he replied, and we understand what he meant. *Never be surprised* is a good motto in public life. Yet again and again we see on television important statements made and fluffed by tired executives after long industry union meetings, or by ministers at the end of night-long sessions in the meeting rooms of Brussels. As I write, the nation was the opposite of impressed by the interviews which the Prime Minister, John Major, gave on his way home from a farewell meeting with the outgoing President, George Bush. It later emerged that Mr Major was suffering both from jet-lag and from the demanding schedule that his brief weekend stop-over at

Camp David had subjected him to. His arguments were consequently less concise, his authority was weakened and the enthusiasm with which he should have been arguing his particular cause, was lacking. A key rule, therefore, is that if you are tired, or suffering from flu or whatever, do not try: get someone else to do it for you. Everyone understands a real reason if it is properly presented. Leaders of all kinds, especially if they have press spokesmen to answer for them, need not capitulate to the never-ending demands of the press corps for the 'personal touch'.

When we ourselves get to the top, it is a sign of the times, and a mark of the media circus in which public figures of all sorts have to operate, that, in our private offices, it is now far from unusual to find that the PR teams, the image crimpers, the press officers and the media handlers, far outnumber the private secretaries and advisers on actual issues of policy and strategy. As leaders, we need more than the dignity of a platform and a smile. Public reputation, once created, sticks, and everyone is a prisoner of their image, no matter how sketchy the real evidence is, as the former Vice President of the United States Dan Quayle learnt to his cost.

Talleyrand's remark about nations ruled by midgets is true of much lesser public, business and commercial life as well. Most of us have experienced the difference between famous people as they are seen on a public platform or on a television screen, and what they are like when we actually meet them. The let-down can be slight or severe depending on how much reality matches image. The same principle holds true for the rest of us. Lower down the social and management and professional scale we can all learn the same things and, with the modern technology of the video, see ourselves as others see us daily in our workplace. My experience of teaching shows how important is the video camera, in showing up what we do well and what we do badly. The monitor screen is like a mirror for you to work in front of. But unlike a mirror, it has a memory which you can jog again and again to make sure that you know what you are doing wrong and that you get it right in future. Provided you can find the detachment to examine your performance in a positive and self-critical manner, and get over the 'Oh my God! What a mess I look!' stage, then you will improve rapidly.

So, does image matter? My answer, derived from the evidence from graduate students and from the many I have seen chosen or rejected for promotion or for some top appointment, is that it matters very much indeed. Take something as simple as first entering an interview room. You are immediately looked at and assessed by strangers. They will make that fifteen-second judgement as you open the door, as you close it behind you, as you walk and take your seat at the green baize table. They will make instant judgements and assessments about your clothes, your hair, your posture, your show of confidence or the reverse. Your handshake, firm, soft, or sweaty, will send off its own signals as much as your choice of tie or whether you have taken care to brush the loose hairs off your shoulders before you present yourself.

Everyone reading this book will have their own experiences to go on. When you think about it, you know that it is true that personal first impressions matter. You know you take to or against colleagues in your workplace, not just because of the way in which they work, but because of their personal habits, their style, their mannerisms, and their degrees of aloofness or familiarity. Again and again, we all come across unpopular people who could, with help, so easily and quickly be put on the right lines, merely by a kindly word, not just about subjects like BO, as in the old advertisement, but, more simply, if told a little truth. They can be quietly advised, and not just when tempers snap, that if they made such and such an adjustment to their make-up and way of behaving, all would be so much better. That is what personal impact is all about.

# SECTION TWO

# Paralanguage and Non-Verbal Communication

*When the eyes say one thing and the
tongue another, a practised man relies on
the language of the first.*

Ralph Waldo Emerson

*You can stroke people with words.*

F. Scott Fitzgerald

*A smile is when both corners of your
mouth go up at the same time.*

Vladimir Soloviev, teaching his
Moscow course on Western
job-interviewing skills.

We have all come across people who have no gift of
language, not even their own, yet who insist on saying
nothing, at great length, badly. We all communicate with
each other, and with a wider world, in a huge variety of
good and bad ways – from a smile, a nod or a wink; by
telephone, letter-writing, faxing; or by giving major public
speeches or publishing books or articles. We add things to
the basics of what we say and write, to make sure we are
not misunderstood. Just as we use an exclamation mark

after we write something surprising, or underline a word to give it more emphasis, so, when we talk, we stress some words, raise the pitch of our voice at the end of a question, or pause dramatically to draw attention to a particular point. Human communication is different from that in the rest of the animal kingdom because of our highly developed linguistic skills, which allow us to pass on to others abstract ideas like time, or complex explanations of our feelings. This linguistic ability also allows us to classify and store a huge range of information inside our heads. But simple verbal and oral communication is dramatically built upon in the conduct of inter-personal relationships. We back up our words with a whole range of devices, which comprise what psychologists call *non-verbal communication* or NVC. Some of this is in-built and unintentional, others we learn or contrive, in order to make our point. Psychologists list types of NVC to include not only 'presence' or body posture, but also our paralanguage, our gestures, our eye contact, our proxemics or how close we stand to each other, right down to and including the way we dress.

Our three candidates for promotion have, for example, their own particular ways of non-verbal communication. Alan Grey is so hesitant and modest in his demeanour, however, that even when he speaks, we barely notice him. John Hustle, by contrast, is annoyingly pervasive. He seems to be everywhere, and tends to go around offices believing he is the life and soul of the party, constantly whistling, cracking jokes, pushing ideas, and consequently disturbing our thoughts and actions with his all-pervading presence. His enthusiasm leads not to effective judgement, but to time-wasting and irritation for all concerned. He gets his body language all wrong because he tries too hard, touching people too often to emphasise his point, standing too close to them, talking far more than listening because he is more enthused by his own ideas than he could ever be by thoughts emanating from others. He is like the typical politician of whom it is said that you can always tell them from the glazed look that crosses their face when the subject of the conversation wanders away from them. By contrast, David Wright judges his timing and his proxemics correctly; he listens well, he speaks with proper authority and only when he knows what he is going to say, and he probably improves his impact by looking at you when he speaks, smiling pleasantly, which adds to his general acceptability. Above all, he gets his timing right and does not interrupt unless he has to.

We will see later how important judging the moment is in all sorts of inter-personal communication and most importantly in public speaking. Some of the best patter-merchants on television are very clever people indeed who know that interviews, for example, whether they be talk-shows or of a more serious dimension, depend on precise timing. By this I do not mean timing imposed by the producers, the cameras, the advertisements and the sche-dules, but the timing in the interview or talk-show itself. People like David Frost, Ned Sherrin and Tim Rice, all highly-educated and thoughtful people, use the might of the pause, not just for the laugh but also because they realise how thought-provoking a well-timed silence can be to us all.

The visual impact of the human communication process is greatly underestimated or ignored by most of us. Frequent studies, not only by psychologists but also by business and time-and-motion consultants, have demonstrated conclusively that, whether between two private individuals or between a speaker and his or her audience, well over fifty per cent of the message is delivered by *the image of the speaker* (their *presence*), just under forty per cent by the character, timbre and strength of the voice, *the elements of sound other than the words*, (their *paralanguage*), and, amazingly, ten per cent or less by the words themselves. Even more cautious studies argue that in two-person conversations, the verbal component of the meaning is only thirty-five per cent against sixty-five per cent for the non-verbal. This seems almost unbelievable, yet it merely underlines the old saying about a look conveying more than a thousand words. After all, we frequently converse without opening our mouths at all. Looks can kill. Any husband and wife, father and child, or angry employer and his or her employee, would agree.

When we speak, we also react to what feedback we receive, all those small clues that tell us if a person or an audience has understood or welcomed what we have said. If, for example, people look puzzled or blank, we realise we have to say more. If they sit upright and alert and intent, or lean towards us rather than avoiding our eyes, we may have their attention. If they slouch, seem bored, or stare vacantly out of the window, we are going to have to spice up our act. If we add a smile to our message, this, in itself, is an enormously important message. We sometimes refer to all this, in general terms, as body language, creating a rapport, or building up an emotional or inter-personal appeal. I will return to this subject later.

---

*Words are, of course, the most powerful drug used by mankind.*

Rudyard Kipling

---

*For I have neither wit, nor words, nor worth,*
*Action, nor utterance, nor the power of speech,*
*To stir men's blood: I only speak right on.*

Shakespeare, *Julius Caesar*

---

First let us look at pure, unadorned language. We only need unencumbered, unaccentuated words to communicate certain straightforward facts or messages like when a train is due to leave a station. We are able to do so, because, if we are speaking the same language, and not Italian or Chinese for example, each word has a commonly understood meaning. It is particularly easy when the words are simple ones like 'table' or 'bed', or 'ten o'clock'. It becomes more difficult with complex terms such as 'infinity' or 'the human spirit', or 'love'. We automatically decode the words or combination of words that others use. We are able to do so because we are born with what some psychologists call an innate *Language Acquisition Device* (LAD) which allows us to learn and absorb such verbal messages. This 'pure' language is all we need for passing on basic information or news. The long-suffering person who recorded the British Telecom speaking clock does not need to inject too much drama into 'At the third stroke, the time sponsored by . . . ', nor does it need emotion to read out the latest stock market figures.

Additionally, between close relatives, a few incomprehensible or half-formed words can be sufficient to communicate a hugely important message, just as, within an office, working colleagues commonly use what has been called 'Company Chinese': curt phrases or expressions that are only used within that organisation to express special internal meanings. Again, a simple admonition like: 'You're late,' can be said with a whole range of meanings, depending on whether it is delivered with fury, with resignation or with a tolerant smile. Alan Grey, our modest and unassuming candidate, probably never gets round to saying enough with or without non-verbal content, to get himself noticed. John Hustle will be so full of the brash words and glib phrases that he, dressed in his shiny, natty gent's suiting and dangling gold chains, will antagonise any serious listener, while David Wright will instinctively adjust his language to his audience, avoiding the use of clichés and unintelligible expressions with those who might fail to comprehend them. He will be much more alert to the reactions and expectations of those listening to him and by his general demeanour and degrees of expressiveness will, in consequence, interact better with them. He has a trained sixth sense which allows him to be at ease with himself and those around him.

From childhood on, as we learn to speak, we recognise other clues to meaning. We will 'read' when our parents are angry or pleased. As adults, we demand human interaction, and don't just say 'eat your food' to a baby in a high chair; we mime the process in the hope of encouraging a sometimes very messy imitation. By this mix of words and gestures we get our message across. Grasp that and we grasp the first step in public speaking. To convince, to persuade, to communicate, it is not just our words themselves that matter, but also things like our degree of eye contact, our facial expressions, our gestures and hand movements, and the general demeanour, which contribute to our spoken message. Sometimes we dispense with words altogether, as when we nod or wink or shrug our shoulders, or give the thumbs-up sign. We force ourselves to look calm and collected in a crisis, or let passion or humour show through as it suits us. We may try to disguise our feeling but the reality often leaks through via uncontrollable aspects of our body language, as when we are highly nervous or afraid or in love.

Of all the above, according to most psychological studies, our eyes win out as the most important avenue for inter-personal contact with, or experience of, something or someone. A person who never looks at us in the eye will thus be classified as shifty or uninterested. Someone who stares too intently can embarrass to the point of forcing us to avoid them at all costs. Someone with a nervous tic or particularly obtrusive physical habits like scratching or nail biting, will offer distractions that diminish the presentation that he or she can make. There are other obvious signals, from a limp handshake through to someone constantly clasping an arm around our shoulders, which can make us feel uneasy and less able to listen or communicate with that person. Think of the sort of person who, whether for short-sighted reasons or not, stands too close to you, or is given to a lot of hand or arm touching to emphasise their point. They may feel that they are establishing a good personal rapport, but it can easily have the totally opposite effect. We each have our own need for a certain body space around us which, if infringed, makes us positively reject another person's approach. While in a normal working environment, this has little to do with sexual attraction, the whole question of communication and body space is additionally weighted, for or against, where there are sexual undertones involved. John Hustle fails to observe the proxemics rule about standing too close to people and constantly touching them unless it is obviously necessary. He will have to be told what a turn-off it is.

People's general facial expressions, the way they move their mouth and lips, also say a great deal about them and what is being said. John Major's 'stiff upper lip' conveys a positive image to bolster even his weaker messages, in stark comparison with what can only be described as the self-satisfied smirk which is the mark of some of his Cabinet colleagues. Some experiments show that up to ninety per cent of the information we get about the external world in general is visual. Thus, if we look brightly and pleasantly at someone while they are talking, they take it as a sign that we are interested; fail to give the right signals, always downcast, brow with a frown, lips and mouth in an apparently disapproving downturn, and they feel uncomfortable. Signalling that we are relating, we find reassuring.

*Good Eyelock Matters.* While John Hustle stands too close, and stares intently at us, while Alan Grey mutters from far away in a corner and never looks us in the eye, David Wright will establish good eyelock, but will not persist with it once he has established the necessary initial rapport.

In addition to all this visual package – of presence, and face and body language – when we communicate, we use our *paralanguage*, to define our words. This provides additional information according to our pitch and tone of voice, our rhythm of speech, our pauses, breathing, volume and base/tenor/alto buttons, our pace and timing, our loudness or softness of delivery. It is the *how* of what is being said. (*Paralanguage*'s definition is sometimes expanded in dictionaries to include all the mannerisms, gestures, and facial expressions as discussed above.) By our paralanguage, however widely defined, we can express lots of different emotions: anger, amusement, admiration, disgust, fear and so on. In 1961, two psychologists analysed this, terming it 'vocal thrust', and found eight distinguishable tones of voice, which corresponded to different moods: affection, anger, boredom, cheerfulness, impatience, joy, sadness and satisfaction. Any actor or actress knows they have to master these patterns of emphasis, in addition to their lines, if they wish to create their characters and make them real. For example, listen to two people talking in a language you do not understand. You can still gather a great deal of information from how they address each other and the tone of the non-verbal messages they convey to each other. Watch a drama on television with the sound turned down, and you will probably get some of the flavour of the plot. A psychiatrist was recently retained by a French newspaper to assess President Mitterrand's body language. This he did, from television, with no sound, and analysed all the raised eyebrows, the hands in constant movement, the eyebrows arched in astonishment or disdain, the expressive waves and the emotional shrugs of the shoulders. By repute, the psychiatrist was able to 'read' a huge amount of message without hearing any words whatsoever, though admittedly the President is widely renowned for his non-verbal expressiveness even in a country where hand gestures are much more flamboyant than in the Anglo-Saxon or Germanic worlds.

Just as facial expressions will tell you things about happiness, sadness, surprise, disgust or contempt, so, if you attempt to voice your views in a dull monotone and try to keep your face totally emotionless, not only will your boredom level be high, but your message is far less likely to get through. Psychological studies have demonstrated again and again how important a lively paralanguage is in putting yourself across to others. To emphasise the point, one such study, in 1972, looked at what happened when people were given a verbal message in a non-verbal style that actually contradicted the message, such as, for example, giving bad news with a wide grin on the face. The results showed that the non-verbal cues had about five times the effect of the verbal ones. If people were given a friendly message in a hostile manner, it was not the words that they took note of, or remembered, or acted upon, but the looks. Thus we all take particular care how we appear or smile or look concerned if we feel some rather delicate message might be taken the wrong way. That study again confirmed that out of the three parts of a message – expression, words and tone of voice – the words were consistently the *least* important of all.

I mentioned touching earlier, but there are a number of symbolic touchings that happen in any society, such as a handshake or a pat on the back. Equally, there are other highly meaningful degrees of bodily contact such as a kiss on the cheek or a punch in the jaw. Again in, say, a doctor/ patient relationship or other types of fairly intimate professional linkage, a certain amount of therapeutic or functional touching has to take place to console, to comfort, or to reassure. By contrast, in a crowded tube, we will go to extreme lengths to *avoid* contact with our neighbours. One particular study of proxemics defines closeness by degree: if you are nearer than one to one and a half feet, you can classify your relationship as intimate. If you are between one and a half feet and four feet, the relationship is still fairly personal, while general 'social' placing in normal circumstances is between four and twelve feet. In public settings, such as while speech-making, the space needed will be twelve feet plus. That is why, when John Hustle stands three feet away from you, you do not particularly like it, and, besides, from that closeness you can discover if he has got halitosis, so you tend to avoid him and his views. Maybe however, he is just shortsighted or comes from a Latinate background, since races nearer the Mediterranean have been shown to stand closer in everyday life than do, say, the Scandinavians.

The scowl, the grimace, the smile, the blank stare, all project their own cues. Standing tall or slouching, our body posture and the shrugs and bracing of our shoulders, the way we move our hands and arms, are partly instinctive and partly nurtured methods supporting our language and controlling our conversation. The instinctive bit is of course both in terms of the person making the gesture and the one receiving it. Posture can be utilised very effectively for conveying interest and acceptance: for example leaning towards the speaker is taken as a sign of attentiveness, while if you turn your back deliberately, the reverse may be assumed to be the case.

If you listen without having an opportunity to see the speaker, this highlights the importance of tone of voice even more. Radio audiences, for example, have of necessity to concentrate much more on the words used, but the paralanguage, the strength or weakness, the monotony or drama of the words spoken, takes on an even more critical role. An interesting example of this is told by Pierre Salinger, President John F. Kennedy's former Press Secretary, about the famous 1960s pre-election television debates between Kennedy and Richard Nixon. After the debates, a poll was taken of how TV and radio audiences had reacted to the two participants. The TV audience overwhelmingly favoured Kennedy, largely because Nixon looked so shifty, badly glistening with sweat and with his notorious five o'clock shadow on his jowls. He appeared untrustworthy by comparison with the apparently clean-limbed Bostonian. By contrast, the radio audience, which was huge in those days, overwhelmingly went for Nixon, since, without his visual drawbacks, he was much the more convincing of the two.

And while on the subject of US Presidential speech-making, how about this light extract, taken verbatim from former President George Bush. His syntax, flow, paralinguistic and physical presence rivalled each other for the bottom rung of his communications ladder. Speaking in August 1992, in his faltering, grandmotherly, reedy voice he proclaimed:

> I see no media mentions of it, but we entered in – you asked what time it is and I'm telling you how to build a watch here – but we had Boris Yeltsin here the other day. And I think my times . . . er . . . um . . . campaigning in Iowa, it's kind of an international state in a sense and has a great interest in all these things – and we had this Yeltsin standing here in the Rose Garden and we entered into a deal to eliminate the biggest and most ballistic missiles and it was almost, 'Ho-hum, what have you done for me lately'. [Sic!]

Try this test. Listen to any politician on radio, then watch them on television. On which medium do they fare better? You will find some whose looks and presence fault them, but whose way of speaking alone redeems their performance. The three individuals whose careers we have been following, similarly give us an example of how people react to overall presence. John Hustle, the brash, pushy, communicator will probably fare passably, right down to his beautifully polished shoes. Alan Grey's personal impact will match his name: he will be colourless in style and appearance or worse, totally indifferent as to how he looks, with hair that badly needs a cut, a suit that has seen better days, and a shirt and tie straight out of one of the drabbest department stores. David Wright by comparison, who has an instinctive style about him, will wear his clothes to match his audience. With him, good taste will prevail. We will follow their progress in matters of dress and bearing in the next section of the book.

Think, as a final example of all this, about how we talk on the telephone. We deliberately say things in an exaggerated way to get our point across; we use stronger changes in our tone of voice, or laugh audibly at the other person's joke to show appreciation, where, if they were present with us, we would merely smile. What does this prove? The total perception we have of other people's impact is a *package*, both visual and audible, which fact ought to give us a valuable insight into how we ourselves can improve our own communications skills.

# SECTION THREE

# Dress and Bearing

> *It is an interesting question how far men would retain their relative rank if they were divested of their clothes.*
>
> Henry David Thoreau

> *A man's style is his mind's voice.*
>
> Ralph Waldo Emerson

> *A well-tied tie is the first serious step in life.*
>
> Oscar Wilde

When the new television station GMTV came on air in January 1993, the Director of Programmes, Liz Howell, talked about the presenters who had been chosen, and why they had been chosen. She came right out with it: 'GMTV is about people looking attractive.' They have to have 'fanciability' she went on. People, audiences, switch on and stay switched on when they 'like' the people they are watching, no matter what they say. They have to look smart and well-groomed as well. Nothing was said by the spokesmen and women for the channel about dynamic news coverage, quality thresholds or safeguarding the cultural life of the nation. It was all about sex appeal and the male/female team balancing out. It was to do with charm and the presenters being, in the words of newsreader Alastair Stewart, 'nice to look at'. That way is the road to large television audiences. Apparently. There is, of course, nothing new in all this. TV presenters around the globe are always well-groomed and well-chosen for their presentability, though, in the past, generally speaking, none actually admitted that they had their jobs merely because they looked good. They were there because they were brilliant and witty. But if advertisers like the 'fanciability' package, where does this leave the rest of us?

We have already got a general impression of how the three exemplars Messrs Hustle, Grey and Wright are getting on: the first dapper, the second drab and the third confidently well-groomed. The latter in particular now fully realises that how he presents himself matters in communicating with a wider world. He is the only one, so far, that would come across passably on television. He also knows that how he looks, and the personal impact he makes, can affect his overall chances of success in working up to a leadership position. Yet he would run a mile from taking part in a serious discussion of what is meant by 'well-dressed', particularly for men. In his experience this seldom takes place outside the pages of the style magazines. He sees the subject as something trivial or irrelevant. He believes that people either have style or they don't. Yet ask him and he will tell you who is going to go further in life: the coherent, well-dressed, well-made-up woman executive, or the dowdy one with a much better CV; the clean-cut man in well-made suits and clean shirts, or the identically qualified one in unpressed clothes and a slept-in hairstyle?

Psychologists apportion a lot of weight to the signals given by various styles of dress (or undress) in interpersonal communication. But how we wear what we wear can also be a great indicator of our state of mind or wish to have an effect. We have to get the balance right, as various great writers of the past have noted. 'The apparel oft proclaims the man,' said Shakespeare, while William Hazlitt warned that, 'Those who make their dress a principal part of themselves, will in general, become of no more value than their dress.' And Bertrand Russell cattily remarked of someone: 'Not a gentleman, dresses too well.' Samuel Johnson, in turn suggested that, 'Fine clothes are good only as they supply the want of other means of procuring respect.' Where then does the truth lie?

Let us go back to basics. We are all familiar with the various uniforms that are used to signal that someone is occupying a particular role in society: a nurse, a soldier, a policeman, a traffic warden, a priest, for example. But other forms of dress may also impart information about the person – someone in a professional job for instance, like a barrister, will tend to dress neatly and in a highly conventional style, while someone in the pop music world is unlikely to be seen wearing a traditional suit except on very special occasions. Charlie Chaplin conveyed a huge amount, and not just to laugh at, by how he dressed, without ever opening his mouth. So by 'reading' the ways that people dress, from off-the-peg C&A to the Savile Row suit, on to jeans and T-shirts, or Salvation Army rejects, or by noting someone's ability to choose a tie that matches, we make judgements which guide us as to how to interact with them. Hairstyles, or handbags, or briefcases, or beards, or plunging necklines, or earrings on men send out positive or negative signals. We all know, though we may not like to admit that we have our judgements seriously affected by such fripperies, that dress is quite often the very first, and often the only thing we notice about many people. While our three candidates for higher office have already learned some of the pitfalls in communication and presentation, they still have a lot to pick up in this regard. John Hustle, with his over flamboyant ties and rather too sleek suits, if he gets the right advice, will be told that he looks a bit too much like a used car salesman to get him the top job in the bank that he has set his heart on. Alan Grey, had he been in the Army would have been told to have a haircut three months ago. He might still be alright in a University or Polytechnic Social Sciences Department, but will not necessarily be considered good partner material by the firm of accountants in which he is currently struggling. He has to learn to ditch that sad and scruffy tie, and understand that collars ingrained with grime, matched with an inch of dandruff on his shoulders, do not immediately inspire confidence and respect in others.

Uniforms say one thing; everyday clothes another, but when we move to the top echelons of life we are particularly affected by the 'dressing up' of status and rank, the panoply that surrounds authority, the trappings that prime ministers, monarchs and presidents all have around them. This might include security guards, private secretaries, courtiers, robes, medals and ribbons, and also, sadly, an officiousness that is discovered not only in grand palaces but also in the outer and inner offices of company chairmen, ministers of the Crown and top people everywhere. The very furniture of high office sends out signals that 'we are in charge'. But, as Shakespeare also said:

> The primogenitive and due of birth,
> Prerogative of age, crowns, sceptres, laurels,
> But by degree, stand in authentic place
> Take but degree away, untune that string,
> And hark! what discord follows . . .

If the Emperor has no clothes, what is really left?

Dress is not just used for puffed up reasons of self or institutional pride, of course. It is also used to command respect and to make the wearer listened to, in rapt attention. Why else, in social terms, do the police and the army, or in other fields, priests and archbishops, or judges, wear such otherwise outlandish and opulent mitres, wigs, robes, and other regalia. Redolent with history, they are deliberate social devices retained to impart awe and reverence, and a sense of the discipline and majesty of authority, both religious and temporal. In times past the same was true of teachers and professors decked out in their mortar boards and gowns, which were worn to add eminence, to make themselves better listened to if not better understood. These are, of course, not the only reasons for the wearing of uniforms or conforming dress: discipline, ease of identification, conformity and other factors all come into the argument as much in adult life as they do over the vexed question of uniforms in schools.

All this reinforces the significance of everyday dress as well. In politics, for example, Neil Kinnock's image advisers, over the decade or so that he was Leader of the Opposition, advised him to move away from casual, light-coloured suits (light, according to psychologists, suggests a lack of seriousness) to the sombre double-breasters he used in his later years. His ties and shirts, like Mr Major's, when he went to 10 Downing Street, also improved dramatically. (Compare this to President Jimmy Carter, who tended to give his famous fireside chats to the American people while wearing a woolly cardigan, prompting the man in the street, who wanted the President to look like a president, to ask, 'who the hell does he think he is?') By contrast, some do not need clothes to make their impact and presence felt. The Queen, because of who she is, is just as compelling in a day dress as in her Sovereign robes.

The danger is that our judgement over how people dress leads us to stereotyping, in which we treat people the same way just because what they wear is similar. This is as true – no matter how careful we may think we are – as how we make judgements by sex, age, race, educational background and so on. We all have shorthand ways of pigeon-holing individuals not so much out of prejudice but due largely to lack of time. There always is a huge amount of information about people that could be made available to us, but life is short. Young people, for example, who adhere to one particular style or fashion, tend to get lumped together and are not seen as individuals, because of their age 'uniforms'. But in everyday business and social life, we make just as many unsubtle assumptions about colleagues and friends because of the suits, costumes and dresses they buy and wear. There are lots of glib expressions around to describe the effect of all this, such as 'power dressing', and indeed there are certain guidelines which should be followed by anyone wanting to impart a message about their would-be role in any group or organisation. Treated lightly though this subject may usually be, our other accoutrements, ties, shirts, jewellery, add to the definition of our status, and signal how we appear to want to be seen by others. We have total freedom to choose what we wear and how we look in order to be accepted by our peers and in order to fit in. Only occasionally will we deliberately get ourselves up in order to stand out from the crowd.

It is not just what one wears, but *how one wears it* that has its effect. A Savile Row suit or an expensive designer dress carries little authority if it is worn with a slouch, or with unkempt, unwashed hair. Mr Grey could disguise many failings by dressing better and standing up straight, but, even then, his negative facial expression may let him down. Posture and general esprit are of major importance; both Mr Hustle and Mr Wright stand up fairly well, but Wright has the distinct lead because his style of clothes, his choice of slightly more traditional designs rather than the sharp-suited high fashion that his colleague likes to flaunt, gives him more universal acceptability.

In considering the effect dress has upon others, it is perhaps worthwhile to look separately at the case of the career woman. How she presents herself – her clothes, her hairstyle, her make-up and so on – takes on an extra special dimension. The male of the species can easily wear the same suit day after day, week after week, maybe only relieved by a subtle change of shirt colour or choice of tie. Indeed were a man to turn up every day in a different style or cut of suit, light coloured, then dark pin stripes, then a heavy tweed, he would be considered rather odd. Women, by contrast, are expected to vary their clothes as much as they can afford, unless they are in jobs where some sort of standard uniform is required. Successful women in business and in politics can go a certain way towards individualistic, high-fashion power dressing, but if they turn up looking like Zandra Rhodes, or in haute couture outfits which suggest they are about to lunch in some hugely trendy restaurant, they will be deemed suspect, not just by their fellow men but by their women colleagues as well. Extremes and extravagances are outlawed. So much is a matter of current convention: for both men and women, clothes, like war paint, send tribal signals to others of the tribe.

Back to politics, let us take the case of Michael Heseltine. Here is someone well-known for flowing locks and a Rambo/Tarzan-type image, a man who delivers extremely well with strong eye contact and an apparent deep conviction in what he is saying. His clothes are well cut and he wears them with distinction. They are part of the package. He has many political critics but there is no doubt that his delivery goes down particularly well, especially in front of large audiences and at party conferences. His rousing speech to the October 1992 Tory party conference was memorable in part because it was one of the few over those four days that actually made the proceedings come alive, but also because of the determination with which it was delivered. If you look at Heseltine's speeches in written form you will see why: he has a tendency to make each sentence a stand-alone statement, well constructed and to the point. As a result he declaims a whole string of interconnected sound-bites which, *backed by his powerful visual presence* and his knowledge that when he stands to speak he is putting on a 'theatrical act', gives him far more instant credibility than John Major will ever have. Having watched in close up, I would also argue that had he delivered Chancellor Norman Lamont's lacklustre speech, which came in the middle of a major sterling crisis, he would have been cheered to the rafters, an event which no doubt would have had its own effect on the exchange rate and in the stock market, where illogical sentiment rules just as much as it does among the financially illiterate. Heseltine looked the leader. Lamont was just a grey man in a grey suit.

Other examples of a package of personality, dress, and looks coming together in an impactful way are found in people such as Lord White, the Chairman of Hanson Industries, and Gianni Agnelli, the Founder Chairman of Fiat. In both these cases their image, and the perception that the world has long had of them, is aided by that distinction which well-contented age brings to certain men. Money helps too. In addition to money, success or power makes its own mark, not just with the opposite sex (in both directions – ask any rich widow) but with a wider world. Incidentally, the former American Secretary of State Henry Kissinger always argued that an aura of power was the greatest aphrodisiac to women and he had plenty of experience to go on.

It is a small step from considering dress and bearing to looking at what has been called the *halo effect*, the discreditable but verifiable tendency for better-looking men and women to be widely perceived, in psychological studies, as more honest, more able, more votable for. Another definition of the halo effect in some text books relates to someone who, being recognised as having one good characteristic or trait, for example, generosity, will also be perceived to be brave or wise or in other ways talented, without any real evidence for this. On the basis of this effect, were it universally true, we would all be ruled by Robert Redford look-alikes, and all public organisations would use stunning actors and actresses, if they were able to read their lines well and convincingly enough, to deliver any important message. Thus the fact that it is only immaculately smooth and convincing communicators who are used to try to sell shampoo or Italian cars or dog food in most television commercials. This is presumably what those executives at GMTV were thinking of in choosing their front men and women, their presenters and newsreaders. Yet, in the long run, looks are seldom enough on their own. Walter Cronkite, who used to be the most revered newscaster and anchor man in the American media, while he certainly looked the part, was also highly intelligent, authoritative and grandfatherly, giving rise to the oft-quoted remark that one did not believe a news item until one heard Walter read it. But, generally speaking, unless you have somehow acquired the well-established 'character' and reputation of a David Bellamy or a Leo McKern, you won't be chosen by the advertising profession to communicate and persuade, let alone to read the news if you are as 'colourfully ravaged' as these two are.

The general physique of our three candidates, their body-size, shape and overall 'attractiveness' will, consequently, influence how they are perceived and responded to. For example, some psychologists suggest that *endomorphs* (that is chubby, well-rounded people – Mr Grey is the closest) tend to be viewed as agreeable, warm-hearted, good-natured and sympathetic, while *ectomorphs* (those of light and delicate build) are people of quite tidy though perhaps tense characteristics. Continuing briefly with the psychological jargon, *mesomorphs* (those with powerfully physical bodies) are likely to be people of an adventurous, forceful, self-reliant and healthy disposition. Height too, is a significant element, particularly when outsiders judge the male of the species. There is a surprising degree of evidence to show that taller men tend to achieve more in western societies in terms of business status and social success. If these qualifications are coupled with a general attractiveness, such individuals, on the receiving end of more positive eye contact, smiles and closer bodily proximity, are seen as still more friendly and interesting. But the good news for the rest of us is that quite a lot of people (and if he worked at it, even Alan Grey could be one of those), despite not being particularly attractive, can override this and become successful and popular with others by developing an attractive interactive style and approach to life.

This leads on to the delicate question of gender and

communication. Do women listen more intently to an attractive man, and vice versa? There is a great deal of psychological evidence, beyond the scope of this book, that suggests that, from an early age, because boy and girl children are dressed and responded to differently, such early experiences contribute to our behaviour patterns to the opposite sex in later life. Female readers of this book may disagree, but there is a lot of evidence to suggest that when addressing others, particularly men, they tend to smile more, require less inter-personal space and touch more, use more head nods and engage in more eye contact than males. For good or bad, women are also perceived, in psychological studies, to be more skilled at interpreting non-verbal behaviour in others. Thus if we introduce three female characters on the Hustle, Grey and Wright lines, all of these will have additional innate factors in their communication skills which will make it easier, in some circumstances, for them to communicate. By contrast, there is a lot of circumstancial evidence to show that an interview panel of men will listen and make judgements about a woman which are not entirely based on merit, marking them down harder if they come in with less attractive physical attributes and/or appear to care little about how they look or dress.

The importance of image looms particularly large when the much discussed subject comes up of 'a woman's place' in the maze which is office or national politics. We are all aware of the common perceptions or misperceptions about women in hierarchical positions. In the typical office, for example, or when competing for advancement, a woman is branded as bright, or attractive, or can type well, or can take dictation, or can handle the word processor, or can bring cups of coffee without being reminded. Too often, in what are still largely male-dominated preserves, that is the sum-total of how much a part they are seen to be able to play in business or professional life. The process of change is slow.

Dress and bearing is important for both sexes. Only occasionally will skill, expertise and experience allow the emergence of less well groomed people like John Cole, the former BBC Chief Political Correspondent, who, despite everything his mimics had to say about his accent, cut through these disadvantages to give wise and thoughtful commentaries on the political events of the day. Mr Cole disproved many rules on dress, since his outside winter gear resembled something knitted by a demented grandmother. His popularity, in part, was because we are a nation that likes the occasional eccentric, which is why we tolerate (indeed they have a strong following) the oddities of delivery by people like the weatherman, Mr Ian McCaskill.

In certain circumstances voice matters more than presence. John Humphries and Brian Redhead have long been the (usually) friendly and familiar presenters of the influential Radio 4 breakfast programme, *Today*. Humphries, a man for whom sleep does not appear to matter, also appears on BBC TV nightly news as a main newsreader, and highly presentable he looks. Brian Redhead, unevenly bearded and usually casually dressed, would on the other hand (and he would probably agree) present an appearance on the small screen that might prove distracting to his viewers and reduce the value of his message, whereas his voice alone gives an amused and authoritative start to the day. He is more a presenter than a newsreader, a thoughtful, and mellifluous companion to the events of the day, in the best Alastair Cooke tradition. Such people have a special quality, and have been chosen for their clarity of diction and listenability of their speech patterns. Their paralanguage follows the other great radio voice traditions of the past, with the dignity, urgency and thought of an Ed Murrow, or Alvar Liddell.

There are certain things you will never be able to do much about. But Alan Grey now realises that as looks are not his strong point, he has all the more reason to work at his posture, dress and overall performance. Size, as I mentioned earlier, can be of benefit if you are tall, though we all end up the same apparent dimensions when we are being interviewed on the television screen. In business dealings, there is no doubt that Lord Hanson's height, at six-feet-five, has been an additional advantage to a very powerful man. General Norman Schwarzkopf, the Gulf War Commander in Chief, was known as both Stormin' Norman and The Bear, and he himself recognised that his build had helped him enormously on his way up through the ranks. It has been suggested that Pavarotti, great voice though he has, has achieved the highest acclaim through an image package that embraces the reputation of his great girth. Cyril Smith, the former MP, would certainly not have been so widely known but for his size. On a less happy note, I have watched people at a glittering reception stand in line waiting to be 'received' by Robert Maxwell, of whom most people stood in great awe. He, a very large man, made an impact and commanded deference both by the booming power of his personality and by fear of the effectiveness of his writs. By contrast, small size has to have real power or aggression or intellect built into it to make its owner's impact felt. History is littered with many well-known examples, from Napoleon to Hitler. Sir Michael Edwardes (five-feet-four) and Lord Beaverbrook had no problem making themselves listened to, respected, or feared.

Messrs Wright and Hustle (and indeed Grey) have no specific upsides or downsides in regard to size. But they, like the rest of us ordinary mortals, can do a great deal to improve their chances of preferment or promotion by looking at what they wear, how they wear it, how tall they stand and how they can make the best of what they've been born with (short of plastic surgery). Individuals and organisations, no matter how informal they may seem, openly or tacitly insist on certain norms of appearance. This was exemplified by the remark, at the time of the last British general election, of Robin Cook, the Labour Party's intelligent and coherent Health Spokesman. He was asked about his future leadership ambitions. Cook, who is reputed to have once described himself as looking like a squirrel with a bad shave, responded that his Party did not have a record of electing diminutive red-bearded Scots to the leadership. Nor, presumably, would the electorate have rallied to the party if they had.

The American cynic Charles Darrow once remarked to friends: 'I go to a better tailor than any of you and pay more for my clothes. The only difference is that you probably don't sleep in yours.' He realised that yellowing shirts and matching teeth don't make a good impression; dandruff on the shoulders is a definite vote-loser. Scruffy donkey jackets, as Michael Foot, the former Labour Leader, found out on his way back from the Cenotaph after a Remembrance Day Service, can do a lot of irreparable damage. Kenneth Clarke, the British Chancellor of the Exchequer, is gradually disposing of his ill-fitting suits and battered suede shoes as he realises that they have become too prominent an object of mockery. Personal grooming may be an expression more commonly seen in male fashion magazines, but personal blemishes can have a devastating effect. In the mid-seventies, as a diplomat in New York, I once had what I believed was going to be an honourable if not too onerous job escorting a number of distinguished visiting British MPs from television studios in Manhattan, to the Senate and Congress in Washington, and on to elegant dinners in Boston and Chicago. Compared to their healthy looking, dandruff-free, well-dressed,

well-polished American counterparts, my fellow country-
men looked a tired, run-down, unwashed and rumpled
bunch of deadbeats, whose occasional charm and sparkle,
and generally superior intelligence, was lost or submerged
by their grey- and white-flecked demeanour. They had
come to persuade or lobby on Northern Ireland or Con-
corde landing rights or some such, and their efficacy was, I
could see, being instantly undermined by the first fifteen-
second judgements of their hosts. Lord Hanson, who had
similar experiences in the past, has always insisted on well
turned-out colleagues and employees, even to the extent of
providing them, both male and female, with hair grooming
treatments in office time. If someone as busy and successful
as he thinks that personal grooming matters so much, it is
worth taking note.

So how do you go about improving yourselves? When
individuals, in my experience, see their recorded performance on video for the first time, their remarks tend to be
about their appearance 'God, what a mess I look.' 'I must
lose some weight.' 'Where the hell did I get that tie?' 'What
a cheap looking shirt.' 'My hairdo . . . ', and so on. The
efficient use of a mere mirror is the first step towards
communication success; the video retains the image for
longer. Narcissism may be a vice; looking closely and
constructively at your image is not.

Let us look, for example, at how the three candidates for
preferment are getting on. They now 'see' how they look,
understand a bit about their positive and negative body

language and about the strengths and weaknesses of their paralanguage. Mr Hustle has been made aware that his super snappy way of dressing and his rather too precise little moustache and shiny, pointed shoes are not the best way to show himself off. Alan Grey has smartened himself up, invested in a haircut and bought a rather better-fitting suit and some new shirts, while David Wright, though initially the most promising of the three, has had to look to his laurels so that the other two do not lap him. They have had some personal tuition in self projection and the video camera has given them time to study their images and to make suitable adjustments. Largely self-taught, they have understood that that indescribably scruffy pair of trousers, that paunch straining at its shirt buttons, the unpolished shoes, the hairstyle that was a total distraction, can all be improved simply and cheaply. Self-tuition has been three-quarters of their battle. To help the process along, I would have invited them to stand up and speak on any subject of their choice for a short time, two or three minutes maximum, and together we would go through their recorded performance, quite often with the sound on the video monitor turned right down at least in the first run through, as this forces them to look more closely at the essentials of their dress and bearing. It is remarkable how much difference a second run through of the same short speech, after a joint teach-in, makes to the overall performance.

This training technique can also be of value to people who

have frequent opportunities to see themselves on television. I constantly meet politicians who have an almost daily opportunity to analyse how they look and how they sound but who are surprised when we play back some of their appearances with the sound turned down. Only then do they concentrate on the visual, which is understandable given that their lives are attuned to hearing words and reacting to them. Advice of a personal nature on how well or badly you present yourselves tends to come from friends or family. For example, we have all, probably, been told that some colours suit us better than others. If you are pale complexioned you need to choose clothes that do not make you appear like ghosts. Colour coding comes naturally to most of us. Dark suits we tend to equate with seriousness and trustworthiness, while light colours match relaxed occasions. Most of us also instinctively know how to dress to suit our characters, how to have style without being flash. We avoid designer clothes if we wish to avoid appearing too opulent or ostentatious; a high-quality, classic style, however defined, for both men and women, may give an impression of slightly old-fashioned staidness, but there is, in most situations, advantage in tending towards the conservative. And the classic costs less in the long run if only because it gets out of date less quickly than the latest fashion trend.

To sum up, clothes, as much as bearing and demeanour, are powerful, unspoken ways of communicating. It is not just what, but how you wear what you wear that counts.

Clothes may be expensive and good but the visual impact will be lost if they are worn with a hang-dog expression and a lack of poise. As Thomas Pink (the shirtmakers) say in one of their advertisements: *You'll never get to the top in a shirt like that.*

Here are some final thoughts:

1. It gives you much more self-confidence and self-esteem if you feel and look smart.
2. Stand tall.
3. If you want to impact an image of control and serious authority then dress more formally.
4. Develop a sophisticated sense bearing by looking at how your peers, seniors and others present themselves.
5. Dress with propriety. Even if there is nothing written down, there are usually unwritten rules – for example, about women not wearing trousers in certain offices. If you want to make a display of yourself do so, but then be prepared to take the consequences.
6. While 'power dressing' may be a gimmicky expression and few positions require a military inspection, the little details – shoes polished, nails clean, clothes pressed and crease free, can make the difference between success and rejection.

# SECTION FOUR

# Public Speaking Skills

> *It's not often that you see a man lose the next general election on prime-time television, but I think it may have happened last Tuesday . . . To the television audience it made a three-sick-bag spectacle. It smacked of indiscipline, sentimentality and one with the image not of a triumphant party leader but of a buffoon . . .*
>
> John Naughton of the *Observer*, commenting on Neil Kinnock speaking, then leading the singing of *We Shall Overcome*, at the 1991 Labour Party Conference in Brighton.

> *Many managers dread public speaking, particularly to their peers . . .*
>
> *Management Today*, January 1992

> *Let thy speech be short, comprehending much in few words*
>
> Ecclesiasticus

Unlike writers, public speakers subject themselves to an immediate test of their words from their audience's reaction to them. Before you stand up to make any public speech, there is an essential list of prior conditions of which you must be satisfied.

These are:


1. That you know your subject.
2. That you know your audience.
3. That you believe in your subject.
4. That you have practised your delivery.

You should never, unless it is absolutely essential, get to your feet if one or other of the above has not been met.

It is widely believed that the art of talking to large audiences is not what it was. Commentators complain that oratory has given way to 'mere talk'. Today, they argue, most political speeches are not great oratory, but tirades against the opposition. Oratory was a subject that, before the advent of mass communication, was something considered worthy of careful study. Books were written about it, teaching was given in it; it was a skill of major political and social significance, something that no person in public life could succeed without. The arrival of television and radio has removed the need for many skills implicit in it as a subject. There has been a gradual process of change. Lloyd George at his feeblest – and *he* was accused by his contemporaries of ruining the art of public speaking – was a paragon in comparison to the drones that today pass for orators in the political debating chambers on both sides of the Atlantic. One only needs to attend any of the party conferences to hear how lamentable is the state of the art, with flat, badly pronounced and cadenced words, drably and emotionlessly delivered. The very different skills of communicating via the electronic media have taken its place.

Even today, listening to a recording of Nehru on Indian independence or the Abdication Speech can still be extremely affecting. Now, however, more profitable careers have attracted many who might once have gone in for politics, which has helped to lower the quality of speech-making in the same way that modern information technology has done away with the need for much direct, face-to-face speech.

Making a serious speech is a serious matter. If you make a bad twenty-minute speech to a hundred people, that is not just twenty minutes of your time wasted, but a total of over two or three days of other people's.

Our three candidates for preferment realise this, but, like most middle managers, they will seldom have to stand up and make a big set-piece speech just yet in their careers. Nonetheless, they are more commonly required to speak aloud to groups of friends or colleagues, or indeed make a sales pitch to half a dozen potential clients around a table, where many of the same techniques are needed. As ambitious executives, they will face increasing demands on their public speaking skills as they progress up through the ranks of life.

Actors spend a great deal of time rehearsing their parts. For the rest of us, our public speaking and other personal impact skills can be radically improved by even a small amount of practice. If you work as hard at your delivery as you do at your text, then you will get a long way. Improving your mannerisms, your voice projection and your confidence is important. Only three other things matter when you stand up to communicate to, or convince others: how you look when you stand up and speak, how you say what you have to say, and what you say. Of the three, as we have seen, the last often matters least. Without rushing off to a charm school or getting hooked on power dressing, or taking up acting, there are many straightforward moves *anyone* can make to better their overall presence and acceptability, either as a messenger or as a leader, in dealing with other people in public. It starts with looking hard at how you appear, even, as I said earlier, if it is only a case of using a mirror to proper advantage. People believe more of what they see than what they hear. Look closely at yourself in the glass. Do you *look* believable?

Nearly seventy per cent of senior managers and decision-takers in a recent British opinion poll said that one of their greatest fears was to have to speak in public. I have seen an incisive and powerful Captain of Industry quake with trepidation prior to going to the podium, and heard a much decorated Army General admit recently that he felt physically sick before making a public speech. Why then is more time not spent on learning to speak well? Unless you go in for debating, it is seldom practised at school or at university. It is not because it is especially difficult to master, since, while no-one can wave a wand and make you into a great speaker, good tuition can make you passably effective. A fumbling, inarticulate shambles of an interviewee can, equally, be turned into someone who, while knowing their limitations, can put a case across without too many problems. My experience of teaching over many years is that huge and rapid improvements can be made. We *can* all learn to speak confidently. We *can* conquer nerves. Both come with intelligent practice.

## Voice and Accent

---

*Mend your speech a little, Lest it may mar your fortunes.*

William Shakespeare

---

Let us look briefly at the question of voice, tone, and accent. One thing you should become fully aware of before you go on stage, is the sound of your own voice. Tape yourself reading from a book or article, and play the result back. Listen carefully. Are you pleased or horrified at the actual sound? Is what you hear gentle or strident, hesitant or resonant, convincing or off-putting? What is your timing and pace like? Are you interesting or boring? If you can take and trust their judgement, what do family or friends really think?

If you ever had an opportunity to listen to Tony Benn or Enoch Powell, despite the fact that they came from diametrically opposite sides of the political spectrum, you would realise why they were both widely acclaimed as two of the best political debaters in the House of Commons. They spoke with quiet reasonableness, with great conviction, and, for the most part, without notes. Their voices were confident and self-assured and I can always remember how Mrs Thatcher, in particular, would sit forward on the front bench and listen intently on every occasion at which Mr Powell stood up to speak. Both were attractive through their presence and their paralanguage. But the content came quickly to the fore, and despite everything I have said about the verbal quota, such were their political views that, for all their debating skills, they lost out in their separate, inevitable way to the extremes of British political life.

Another interesting political example, though more of the bully-boy school of public speaking, is that of Dennis Skinner MP, the so-called Beast of Bolsover. He, when he speaks in the House of Commons, adopts an erupting volcano style, blasting forth with emotion, seemingly unable to speak quietly and in measured tones about anything. Spitting rocks and lava both in and out of the House, he is the classic case of a speaker who would never need a megaphone. He is much admired for his vigour, determination, humour, and unswerving hold to the policies in which he believes. But such a manner of speaking is better suited to the rough and tumble of the hustings than to the House, which emphasises the need to suit words and style to the audience you are addressing.

At the outset, with no particular training and a distant memory of a school-teacher once telling him he was too clever by half – which at the time he thought was a compliment – John Hustle is perfectly capable of making a glib, pushy speech, with a fair amount of contrived humour of the joke-telling variety built into it. But his style is more that of a bar-room stand-up act than of someone delivering a serious message. Alan Grey will receive little attention; his audience's minds will wander almost immediately, because he, if not inarticulate, thinks nothing of reading his speech, and rather badly at that, in a dreary, unmodulated, and hard to hear voice. He is some-one who would be far better off handing out copies of his text for the audience to read, since it may be quite well-written, rather than wasting both his own time and that of a room full of others. David Wright is a moderately good speaker, has a reasonable pitch and ability to project his voice, but still delivers a fairly formal and wooden perfor-mance, since, once he gets to the lectern, the good natured ease for which he is privately well-known, and which, with a little training, he can be taught to bring out, seems to desert him.

Only Hustle will fall into the temptation of trying to inject some humour. At best, and we will return to this later, it can be a great stimulator of attention, not so much in the traditional, joke-telling mode as in the quiet, incisive, or wickedly cynical approach. Lord Carrington was a politician whose wry sense of the absurd underlined almost everything that he said, while John Smith, at his best, is dangerous to those sitting opposite him across the despatch boxes because he gets the Tory Party backbenchers to laugh with him. Denis Healey also had this skill: mockery and dismissive remarks such as the dead sheep gibe about Geoffrey Howe, made him a parliamentary legend, and modern books of quotations are full of his witty maxims and humorous remarks.

When I suggested listening carefully to your own voice on tape, it was because we all react either negatively or positively to voices that we find insipid, harsh or pleasing. When I was helping set up Melody Radio, London's all-music station, I learned how important it was to their easy-listening style, and to their audience, to get announcers with the right sort of voices. If you listen to a lot of radio you appreciate that a voice that suits a pop music station will hardly give the required authority for a news reader or a political commentator on BBC Radio 4. In day to day living, we react very differently to voices, irrespective of what is being said, that suggest power or weakness, that seek to persuade, that are querulous, kindly or bad tempered.

In the area of public speaking, women especially can have difficulty with their public voice, their paralanguage. Too often, what might be considered 'authoritative' comes out sounding strident or screechy, while too soft a voice merely ends up suggesting weakness. It is particularly difficult for a woman's voice to hold the attention of a mixed audience, for instance as an after-dinner speaker. The mix of gravitas and lightness that is required is often difficult for women to master. Even someone as professional as Margaret Thatcher, with a very 'caring' voice, deliberately adopted by her, is successful at one level, but at another it sounds merely contrived. Edwina Currie's voice is powerful enough but it provoked widespread accusations of shrillness, largely perhaps because of her forceful content. Margaret Beckett's voice projection (and indeed her overall presence) still lacks the authority that her Shadow Cabinet role demands. Perhaps, among current women politicians, Virginia Bottomley succeeds best, producing the right mix of warmth, determination and overall listenability.

Good pronunciation depends on the ear of the listener. In Britain, Received Standard English and Received Pronunciation, the particular pronunciation of British English which, to quote the dictionary definition, is generally regarded as being least regionally limited, most socially acceptable in educational and status terms, and considered 'the standard', is undoubtedly most valuable if you are putting across a message to a national audience. It might, however, only provoke mirth or derision in a Glasgow or Liverpool pub, or coming from the mouth of the average football team manager or coach. By contrast, in the Home Counties broad Glaswegian or Liverpudlian would be considered, at best, quaint, and would certainly not be considered as an authoritative and persuasive way of speaking. Curiously, surveys show that certain moderate Scottish, Yorkshire, Irish and West Country accents are more widely acceptable. Other strong regional accents (the north-east and Manchester and Cockney seem to suffer) travel badly, and elocutionists are much more in demand in such areas. But even moderate regional accents are sometimes believed by their owners to be something of a handicap: thus Mrs Thatcher's well-documented move away from both the Grantham accent and the vocal timbre of her youth. This author claims no abilities in the direction of easing people away from the accents they were brought up with, but there is no doubt that to have a wide personal impact, the closer you can get to Received English and Received Pronunciation, the better.

Our three candidates, Hustle, Grey and Wright all have perfectly good or perfectly acceptable accents, though Hustle tends to throw in glib pieces of colloquial jargon which do not travel particularly well. In that he is in some ways similar to Alan Grey, who bores for Britain not just by his flat voice tones, but by larding his speech with far too many facts and figures and complex subordinate clauses. He thinks in an intelligent but complicated way and this is carried through to his speech. One way of comparing their abilities is to ask them and people like them to read aloud some great passage of English literature or from the bible. In terms of the effect on the average listener, traditional language and moving words, even when not particularly well read, carry and retain a remarkable authority, while modern usage and turns of phrase, even well read, do not have the same impact.

Similarly, many recent critics of the BBC World Service have argued that a sizeable part of its overseas audience has been alienated following a gradual decision to allow various extreme regional accents to be broadcast in the place of standard English in received pronunciation. One sees the arguments for projecting the splendid variety of the English tongue, but tricky internal British differences are paraded across the airwaves of the world at the expense of a wider understanding by people who have a less than perfect knowledge of that language.

In the USA, equally, despite the much-professed egalitarian nature of its society, accents can also matter very much. For good or for ill, surveys show that the New England upper-class accent has a wider appeal and credibility that the deep southern accent still fails to achieve. President Clinton may of course change all that. The New York Jewish accent or a Mid-Western drawl – these say different things to different people in the USA, because so many of their citizens are first generation American. Foreign accents are by no means a bar to high office, however, as Henry Kissinger so amply demonstrated. If accent really mattered in international affairs, was it not odd that he spoke English with a much more guttural Germanic voice than Willy Brandt, the German Chancellor of the day, who spoke a gravelly *basso profundo* English that was far more perfect, far more universally understandable, than the American's could ever be.

# Your Audience

> *The object of oratory is not truth, but persuasion.*
> Thomas Babington Macaulay

At a recent dinner in London, two hundred of us listened in rapt attention to ex-President Nixon making a speech. He was, at the time of delivery, in his late seventies. He was a man of whom we had all heard so much, and about whom it had been said that one never believed anything until he had denied it twice. Yet here he stood before us, a very senior British audience, and spoke for some thirty minutes with a well pronounced, humorous and interesting delivery, giving us his views of the world situation without a single note before him. He was not just giving some speech he had made a thousand times before, because it was filled with very specific historical British references; he quoted Burke and Canning, and reminisced about his dealings with Gaitskell and Bevin and others from his earliest years of transatlantic politics. He, this discredited ex-President, gripped his audience in a way I have seldom experienced anywhere else at any other time. His audience had started listening with negative, preconceived ideas, but he had rapidly changed them. Nixon had our measure. He knew who we were. Before you get to your feet, you too must know your audience.

Generally speaking, that audience, whoever they are, will make an instantaneous judgement about you and will be biased pro or ante you before you open your mouth. They will look, they will listen, then they will analyse. The first fifteen-second view of you will probably stick. Any public speech has, therefore, to be handled like an actor handles his role; it is a public performance, with an inbuilt 'entertainment' factor. Whether you are giving a short impromptu talk, a lecture, or a major after-dinner speech, this will always be true. You are on parade, to be praised or criticised as much for your delivery and impact as for your content. At the outset, therefore, you have to prepare your ground well. You need to know precisely what kind of audience you are to address. Is it fairly heterogeneous or is it a highly varied one made up of people with differing attitudes, aspirations and expectations? Do they know each other? What are they expecting? Why should they listen to you? The one piece of good news is that *most* audiences are benign.

Your audience will seldom be totally uniform. Take, for example, the Chairman of a large company who is to make a public statement, say, at his company's Annual General Meeting. He (or she) will be talking to a group who have one thing in common: an interest in the financial health of the company and a desire to be there. But, after that, whatever he may think, he is going to be listened to by a wide range of different audiences:

- His or her peers and fellow directors
- The management
- Employees
- Customers
- Institutional investors
- Other shareholders
- City analysts
- Financial press
- Non-financial media/opinion formers
- The public at large

All these may well have different expectations and reactions to what is said. The more uniform the audience, the easier it is to target them effectively.

You may set out by believing that your audience is fairly heterogeneous, and, by and large, if they are all gathered together in one room, they have something in common that brings them together. But you must never take for granted that the various individuals have the same priorities. This is particularly true if you try to illustrate your speech with anecdotes; for example, ones that go down well in a London audience may have little or no interest or relevance if paraded in the north-east or in Scotland. Americans call such pitfalls 'beltway illustrations', ones that fail to carry outside the ringroad that circles Washington DC. And while sexist jokes may pass muster in an all-male environment, they will result in rejection or worse in front of a mixed group of listeners.

The importance of knowing your audience can be illustrated by the case of Arthur Scargill during the miners' strike. When he was talking to a mass of cheering miners at a pithead, he failed to realise that while he might be acclaimed as a hero by those standing directly before him, he was perceived as a dangerous fanatic or demagogue by those whose only experience of him was via the small screen. His opposite number, Sir Ian MacGregor, who was Chairman of British Coal at the time, was, by contrast, totally incapable of communicating to a large audience. He may have been skilled at running the coal business and working in smoked-filled rooms, but his public utterances were a disaster. More recently, and the laws of libel restrain me from giving contemporary examples, the Chairmen of a number of public sector bodies may have been well chosen in terms of running their organisations, but as far as communicating with their key audiences, their market, their consumers and a wider public, they have been remarkably ill-selected.

Politicians, like the rest of us, come across well to one audience, but badly to others. If we look again at the Labour Leader, John Smith, he is usually a competent enough parliamentary performer, someone who is often devastatingly good across the despatch boxes, but who is much less convincing at haranguing a party conference or staring at us through his over-large glasses out of the television screen. By comparison, his colleague, John Prescott, fails to appeal in Parliament, but is a well-respected bruiser in front of a huge party audience. John Hustle will, likewise, probably do rather better in front of a big, not too serious, audience, because he has the quick, glib, attention-grabbing performance style that appeals in a large dimension. It is in front of smaller groups that he will meet his serious critics. By contrast, Alan Grey would, if he ever had to, leave the podium of a great conference hall unheard, but might just gain some respect for what he says when faced around a table by a small group of his equals. David Wright could learn a little from both of them, even though he is still the best of the three in front of a general audience.

# Pre-Preparation

*What the country needs is less public speaking and more private thinking.*

Roscoe Drummond

Like football teams, we all prefer to carry out difficult tasks in familiar, 'home' settings, because it makes us more confident. Having identified your audience, the next step is to familiarise yourself with the territory in which you are going to have to perform. You must case the joint. While for practical reasons you may not always be able to achieve this, the more familiarity you can gain about the conditions and the surroundings you will meet, the better. You should insist on testing the acoustics, the microphone, since even in the best regulated settings, you can experience feedback whine and so on. Your voice is, after all, an instrument which has to be in tune with its setting. Even the most experienced speakers go through this check. Those, by contrast, who come in and then begin by asking if people can hear them at the back, or by indulging in a teach-in game with the audience, over whether the audio visual aids can be seen and so on, have prepared badly, are wasting time and are letting themselves down. W.H. Auden, starting a lecture in a large hall, gave the ultimate warning on all this: 'If there are any of you at the back who do not hear me, please don't bother to raise your hands because I am also nearsighted.'

Some people scrape by with little pre-planning followed by an atrocious presentation, but that is usually in front of colleagues at in-house conferences, and because they are popular in other, social ways. The problems arise when you have to communicate, in an alien environment, with a less tolerant outside world.

Here is a first quick check list of things to consider before even opening your mouth to speak.

1. How big is the room? This is important in terms of the intimacy, or the converse, of your message, and the volume and speed at which you are going to have to deliver. The larger the room, the slower must be your pace.

2. How near will people be to you? Are all the front rows likely to be empty (a common experience) or will they be sitting so close that they can read your notes? After one recent speech where I had noticed that someone who was sitting close to me was reading my discarded notes, I was later asked by him why I had left one particular section out.

3. The microphone: does it work without adjustment/ whining? They frequently don't work first time, even if they have been tested again and again. Is it unidirectional – ie must you speak right into it? Is it at the right height? A microphone can be a hindrance and my own recommendation is to try to do without one if you can. Never go on stage and then have to spend the first few moments adjusting the height and angle.

4. The height of the lectern if there is one: will your notes stay on the gradient? Will you be entirely hidden from your audience the way the Queen was during her 1991 visit to Washington, where only her hat could be seen? Pre-position your notes on the lectern if you can be sure they will be left undisturbed until you get there.

5. Is there water to hand? Even the most experienced speakers get dry mouths. Remove bulky objects and small change from your pockets to be as unencumbered as possible.

6. What is the lighting like? Will it blind you? If they dim the lights when you stand up to speak, will you be able to read your notes? Where are you to sit prior to and after the speech? Will you have to stumble up and down in the dark?

7. The audience? Will it be lively or soporific? How big is it? Could it be hostile or even slightly inebriated, depending on the time of day. Are they all there to be informed, persuaded or entertained? What are their age and sex? Are they largely seated straight in front of you or spread at a hundred and eighty degrees, thereby requiring you to do a lot more looking to left and right to establish a rapport and include them in what you are saying.

8. If you intend to use teleprompts, monitors or reflective glass cue screens, have you practised enough with them to feel totally confident?

9. Who are the other speakers? Are they likely to conflict, overlap, outshine or steal your jokes or your punchlines?

10. Finally, what precisely are you hoping to achieve? What effect do you want to have? *Don't even enter the room until you are entirely clear about that.*

# Coping with Nerves

*I became a good speaker as other men
became good skaters: by making a fool of
myself until I got used to it.*

George Bernard Shaw

*The human brain starts working the
moment you are born and never stops until
you stand up to speak in public.*

Sir George Jessel

Stage fright is commonplace. Many highly successful, professional actors are physically sick before their opening night. Apprehension is not always a bad thing since, for many of us, it gets our adrenalin working and puts us on a high. You may feel much more nervous than you appear. Too many 'ums' and 'ers' can, for example, be a mark of unpreparedness rather than nerves or uncertainty. I do not believe that anyone is entirely free of nerves before making a public speech. Even those two great rivals, Edward Heath and Margaret Thatcher, admitted to having them, particularly prior to that most testing of all political occasions, Prime Minister's Question Time. No book can teach how to beat nervousness, but one way to start is to try to identify the actual roots of the problem.

In this context, Peter Bull, a psychologist at York University, seeks to interpret the mannerisms of leading politicians. He has, for example, taken a look at the Prime Minister, John Major, and reckons that the slightest mention of the name Michael Heseltine is enough to send him into a flurry of gesticulation, perhaps brought on by nerves. 'Whenever the subject of Heseltine came up during a recent interview, Major lost his synchronisation, he would gesticulate all the time and his movements would not match the pitch of his voice,' Bull is reported as saying. 'This is a sure sign of unease.' It certainly illustrates an important point that if you feel nervous, it can be as much due to peer pressure as what your opponents might do or think.

I recently came across another example of great unease when I was teaching a highly intelligent senior public figure how to improve his speaking style. Although he was someone so used to being on the public platform, he admitted to suffering from constant attacks of nerves. One of the reasons for this became quickly apparent: he was large and heavily overweight, yet he continued to try to squeeze himself into a suit that had obviously fitted him in his leaner and fitter youth. This, and the fact that his collar size was an inch or so less than his neck, made him look unrelaxed, hot, sweaty and bursting out all over. He could scarcely fasten his single-breasted jacket and when that button eventually popped open, the shirt beneath it also strained to bursting point over his portly figure. I gently pointed out that all this could be rectified at a stroke by buying a much larger suit, if losing weight was not a real option. He has acted on my advice and if his nerves have not been entirely calmed, at least they no longer show.

The first step in controlling your nerves, therefore, is to isolate exactly what you are afraid of. Among the most common causes, ask yourself if it is –

1. Fear of peer group mockery?
2. Fear of drying up?
3. Lack of knowledge of the subject?
4. Fear of being boring?
5. Fear of losing your audience's attention?
6. Fear of generally making a fool of yourself?

While relaxation techniques also cannot be taught from a book, the following are key methods of reassuring yourself and asserting your own personal mastery of the occasion.

1. Arrive well in advance. Totally familiarise yourself with the location. *This is your turf.*
2. Keep remembering that *you* know more than anyone in the audience about what *you* want to say. Confidence comes most easily from a total mastery of your subject.
3. Remember that you are in control of the occasion.
4. Pre-relax your body. One common method is to stretch, tense and relax your shoulders, then do the same with your arms, ending by flopping then to your sides. Gently continue to shake your arms to remove rigidity and tensions, letting them go limp before you

stand up to speak. Avoid hyperventilating by practising deep, regular breathing rather than going for short, nervous breaths. *Feel yourself into control.*

5. When you stand up, speak slightly louder than you might otherwise do. Speak with authority. The sound of your own loud, confident voice can actually build that confidence. In teaching, I get my nervous clients to speak very much louder than they want, almost bellowing, so that they can both assert their confidence and 'hear' the sound of their own potential vocal power.

6. Never use alcohol to relax. You may think it helps. By and large it does not.

7. Speak as naturally as possible. Anyone who has subjected themselves to listening to a lot of public speeches knows about the special 'speech voice' which many would-be orators adopt. They think it makes them sound more authoritative. It usually ends up being ponderous or contrived. As I said earlier, listen to your own voice on tape. How does it sound? Don't attempt to disguise your accent unless it is so pronounced that it could interfere with the audience's understanding.

8. If there is a lectern, hold lightly but firmly onto its sides. It stops handshake. Focus on one or two sympathetic figures in the audience.

9. Keep your speech short.

10. Keep your speech as light as possible, commensurate with the subject. Pomposity kills.

# The Content of your Speech

---

*Never rise to speak till you have something*
*to say; and when you have said it, cease.*

John Witherspoon

---

*Sheridan once said of some speech, in his*
*acute, sarcastic way, that, 'It contained a*
*great deal both of what was new and what*
*was true; but that what was new was not*
*true, and what was true was not new.'*

William Hazlitt

---

After the initial formalities, any speech, even a fairly light-hearted one, must begin with an explanation of what you are going to say. There is never any down-side in making your agenda clear from the outset.

As to the main content, a speech must have a nub, a fulcrum, a heart, backed up with a few powerful illustrations and some memorable key phrases. Preachers get your attention by telling a story, a parable, which leads on to the main message of the sermon. You can illustrate your argument in a similar way. Because all audiences, and not just congregations, are lazy and need reminding, you can also inject a certain amount of repetition towards the end. Telling them what you have told them never comes amiss.

But the crucial thing as far as the content of any speech goes is to know what is expected. So often a speaker turns up ill-briefed or ill-prepared and eventually leaves a bored or disappointed audience behind. Be clear whether you are meant to be entertaining or advocating some cause, or is it to be a bit of both? In one of his famous letters to his son, Lord Chesterfield advised him that people prefer to be entertained than informed, the latter carrying with it the implication of ignorance or stupidity. Never begin, as many do, with *any apologies* for your content, your subject, your style or anything else. As someone once said, 'Why doesn't the person who stands up and says, "I'm no speech-maker", let it go at that instead of giving us a demonstration?'

I have been at numerous occasions, some of them extremely embarrassing, when the speaker has arrived and either misunderstood or underestimated his or her audience. Lord (Cecil) Parkinson, for example, some years ago addressed one of the great annual dinners in London at which the two hundred guests were every one of them a household name. He had been badly briefed and his consequent stream of platitudes were, for them, tedious, and for him, highly damaging to his reputation. The following year the guests of honour at the same annual dinner were the joint figures of Ronald Reagan and Margaret Thatcher, both of whom had just left office. In their set-piece speeches while in office they tended to be concise and to the point, and their delivery, if not always of the highest oratorical standards, was very competent. On this occasion, they showed their sudden lack of staff, and both subjected us to the sort of long, rambling discourses that their previous private offices would have sharply clipped to size. By contrast, ex-President Jimmy

Carter, who is not generally considered to be a great speaker, came to yet another one of these famous dinners and held his audience very well indeed, not so much through his paralanguage as by the patent sincerity of his message which was largely about his organisation's humanitarian work to alleviate suffering throughout the third world.

## Full Text or Notes

---

*If you want me to talk for ten minutes, I'll come next week. If you want me to talk for an hour, I'll come tonight.*

Woodrow Wilson

---

*I have no time to prepare a profound message.*

Spiro T. Agnew

---

All speeches are important. Even the briefest ones. Churchill realised this and indeed was once accused by F.E. Smith of 'spending the best years of his life working on his impromptu speeches'. Professionals disagree over whether you should work from a full text or notes. My advice is unequivocal. For major occasions, unless or until you are a true professional, there is no doubt that you should prepare a full text to fall back on. In any event, there may be press or public relations reasons for having a substantial text available to issue afterwards. But it should be a text that is, first of all, written for speaking, and not for reading. For speaking, we do not need perfect prose, nor complete sentences, nor exact subordinate clauses. We can allow ourselves greater repetition of the spoken word, because even an alert audience needs more time to assimilate facts that they hear as opposed to one that they read. It should be a text that is not too complex, that is not a mere list of key issues or points. Your speaking style can be varied and fragmented, and yet successful; it can lack perfect smoothness yet deliver a punch; it can be memorable without being too polished and grammatical. You should, however, never read from such a text if you can help it. It is an insult to the audience and is really only permissible where it is more a factual lecture than a speech, or where the precise words need to be strictly adhered to.

The best speeches are never written in text-book style, with verbs precisely placed and independent clauses neatly located in correct order, as if waiting for the teacher's red ink. It is the difference between literature and the spoken word. Quite apart from anything else, if you are a good speaker you may ad-lib or react depending on the mood of the audience and its shift of mood as you progress. Few speeches, therefore, as Brian MacArthur has pointed out, read well after the event. He reminds us of Geoffrey Howe, the former Foreign Secretary, whose famous resignation speech in the House of Commons held not only his fellow

Members spell-bound, but also the nation. This was largely because it was so much out of character for Mr Howe to speak in any degree out of line. It is only when one remembers the mood of that occasion, that a reading of the text would bring his gentle words to dramatic life.

Once the full text of a speech is prepared, everyone has their own methods of progressing. I advocate summarising its main points on eight-by-five-inch cue or index cards (not sheets of paper which are clumsy, and, if you are nervous, will flutter and exaggerate any hand shake) each of which contains one major point or phrase. That point should, if possible, not run over from one card to another. An alternative is to underline or highlight with a yellow marker key words or phrases on the full text itself, which will give you a steer without, hopefully, tempting you to read from that text itself. Nothing turns an audience off more than reading; their attitude is that if you're going to do that, why not just run off copies and hand them out and let them get on with dinner.

The three candidates for top billing are now getting much better in their public performances, but Alan Grey still suffers from nerves and believes that it is better to cling to the crutch of a written text. John Hustle, unable to contain the flow of his words, amuses his audience for a brief moment then starts to bore by parading his self-perceived skills for far too long in front of an increasingly unimpressed audience. David Wright has mastered the cue card technique and while he may 'um' and 'er' a bit too much, his overall performance has a natural, if still too undynamic flow about it.

# Being Introduced

---

*The relationship of the Toastmaster to the Speaker should be the same as that of the fan to the fandancer. It should call attention to the subject without making any particular effort to cover.*

Adlai Stevenson

---

No introduction of a guest speaker should be longer than two minutes, and preferably shorter. Following the introduction – either by the Chairman of the occasion or by the toast master – it is important to be reasonably formal in return, at least in one's opening remarks. There is never any down-side in working one's way around the principal members of the audience on the lines of 'Chairman, My Lords, Ladies and Gentlemen, Lord Mayor', or whatever. Someone who moves straight to the platform and begins his speech without introduction loses a certain degree of respect. It is better to begin, without being over pompous on the lines of, 'Thank you for that highly generous/inaccurate introduction.' I sometimes lead with some other light remark such as, 'Far be it for me to reject such undeserved praise,' or 'After that introduction I can hardly wait to hear what I have got to say,' which, if properly delivered, can get an initial laugh which helps you, first of all, to gain a rapport, and secondly, to build your own confidence by hearing a first friendly reaction from the audience. Here, as always, one has to be sure of that audience, otherwise such remarks can merely lead to an accusation of being facetious.

## The Delivery Itself

---

*After-dinner speaking is the art of saying nothing briefly.*

Edmund Fuller

---

*The right word may be effective but no word was ever as effective as mighty timed pause.*

Mark Twain

---

*Say what you have to say and the first time you come to a sentence with a grammatical ending – sit down.*

Sir Winston Churchill

---

There are a number of simple things to remember about your actual delivery. If some of them repeat what I have said above, it is because they are worth repeating.

1. Create the right impact as you walk to the lectern or stand up to speak. You know what you want to say. Stand there with authority. Look around slowly. Wait until all superfluous noise, such as the clatter of waiters clearing away dishes or serving coffee, is at a minimum.

2. Eye-swing from left to right round your audience. Pick out one or two faces and keep returning to them. It helps you personalise your delivery and develops trust on both sides.

3. Your formal opening should be delivered slowly to gain attention. 'Mr Chairman, Ladies and Gentlemen', etc. Wait for silence to fall.

4. You are there to make them like you. You have to try to entertain in order to convince, winning audience as well as argument. If you see people falling asleep in front of you, you have a problem.

5. Your expression matters. Try, if not to smile, to keep a pleasant expression. We all look more attractive when we smile.

6. The more practising you do, with friends or with a video camera, the better. It is, generally, nonsense to think you can over-rehearse.

7. Make sure you are easily heard. Speak rather too loudly than the reverse. *Speak so that the back row can hear clearly*.

8. Personalise your text. Get someone with experience to run through your text with you and listen to you.

9. Keep it short. Almost no speech should be longer than ten minutes, particularly after dinner. A long speech buries any message.

10. Watch your chosen figures in the audience (see 2, above), their reactions, and their body language, as you progress. Good, momentary eyelock on them will help you focus your speech.

11. Never (I repeat without apology) be tempted to slip into reading from your prepared text halfway through. This is a common fault, particularly, for example in government ministers who may, from previous experience, be able to set their personal mark and fluency at the beginning of a speech. But they then have to plunge into a long and complicated argument, prepared by their civil servants, which, because of the time factor or because of the detail it contains, will be so complex and unfamiliar to them as to make their reading the text almost compulsory. Then, at the end, they jump back to their highly personal style.

12. Do not go too fast. Watch gabbling or swallowing words, or running them into each other. The larger the audience, or the greater the room, the slower you have to speak.

13. Ralph Richardson argued that, 'The most precious things in speech are pauses.' There is an art in their use for effect, for emphasis, and to gain attention. They can be the most dramatic thing in your whole

performance. They can catch the attention of the audience, especially if they are slightly too long. (But not so long that they think you have dried up or lost your place.)

14. Speak, look down and consult your notes, look up, then speak again. That means you should speak only when you are looking at your audience, not when your eyes are staring down at your text or notes.
15. Do not try to memorise the whole thing. It can so easily let you down.
16. Do not ad lib unless you are really experienced.

# Hands

---

*A trembling hand like a clenched fist can speak volumes.*

Anon

---

What you do with your hands is a subject in itself. The only rule is that there are no rules. I tend to hold lightly onto the lectern if there is one, until I get the feel of my speech, my confidence, and my audience. Once gained, I try using simple, confident gestures to emphasise my words. Never put your hands in your trouser pockets: it looks too laidback, if not slovenly, and folding your arms tends to look rather odd or defensive while clasped behind the back can give you too military a flavour. The old fashioned hooking of thumbs into the arms of a waistcoat looks odd nowadays; women don't generally have that option in any case.

One of the most effective speakers in British political life is the Defence Secretary, Malcolm Rifkind. He, like a number of other Scottish MPs, comes from the great Scottish tradition of Edinburgh and Glasgow University trained advocates who tend to be skilled in the art of public oratory with all the gestures and body language that go with it. Rifkind is particularly good in that he can speak for twenty minutes or so, either on a very serious subject or – much more difficult – on a light-hearted one without recourse to notes, without repeating himself, without losing his way and, most importantly, without losing the attention of his audience. His speeches have a beginning, a middle and an end and a constant flow of good-natured humour which tends to give him ten out of ten for listenability. But he also gets his hand and body movements right, moving hands and arms to give emphasis, in the right time scale, to the general flow of his words.

# Length

---

*Always be shorter than anybody dared to
hope.*

Lord Reading

---

*Let thy speech be short, comprehending
much in few words; be as one that knoweth
and yet holdeth his tongue.*

Bible: Ecclesiasticus

---

*Be sincere, be brief, be seated.*

Franklin D. Roosevelt

---

*I've never thought my speeches were too
long; I've always enjoyed them.*

Hubert Humphrey

---

Mr. Humphrey may have done, but, the Lord's Prayer, The
Twenty-Third Psalm and Lincoln's Gettysburg Address are
all less than 300 words long. The last of them took two
minutes to deliver. It is possible, therefore, to be brief and
have an effect. Lord Birkett played it for laughs, but he had
a message when he said, 'I do not object to people looking
at their watches when I am speaking. But I strongly object
when they start shaking them to make sure they are still
going.' Or as Rab Butler remarked, 'An after-dinner speech
should be like a lady's dress; long enough to cover the
subject and short enough to be interesting.'

After one particularly long and boring speech, I remember the person who had been chosen to thank the speaker standing up and saying the following: 'In thanking the previous speaker, I am reminded that any speaker has the attention of ninety per cent of the audience in the first five minutes of a speech. After ten minutes even a good speaker retains the attention of only fifty per cent, while the minds of the other fifty per cent will, if not befuddled by drink, be elsewhere. After twenty minutes, only ten per cent are still listening, and the remaining ninety per cent are miles away, usually indulging in some sexual fantasy. I would, therefore, like to thank the previous speaker for giving so many of us such innocent pleasure.' That says it all. Always be briefer than is required.

# The Art of Speechwriting

---

*He is one of those orators of whom it was well said, 'Before they get up they do not know what they are going to say; when they are speaking, they do not know what they are saying; and when they sit down, they do not know what they have said.'*

Winston Churchill
referring to Lord Charles Beresford

---

*Washington . . . both esteems and dislikes writers, a city of powerful men who are often inarticulate and who dislike being reminded of their condition by the presence of a pale and nervous Wordsmith.*

Peggy Noonan (Speech-writer to
both Presidents Reagan and Bush)

---

The recent political history of the western world owes much to its speech-writers, and many political heavyweights – Douglas Hurd, Chris Patten, Theodor Sorensen and others – have started off in this apparently lowly task. In the Bush Administration, as well as Peggy Noonan, there was one such key figure, William Kristol, who was widely known as 'Dan Quayle's brains'.

There are twelve guidelines, additional to those given above, on which any good speech-writer tends to rely.

These are:

1. Put in a punchy opener. Correct forms of address are always important.
2. Develop the main theme with a beginning, middle and end.
3. Illustrate the theme with a human interest story.
4. Personalise the message. Talk about things from your and your audience's point of view. The use of 'I', 'you', 'we', tends to bond audience and speaker.
5. Develop a relevant sub-theme.
6. Remember the difference between words and sentences that are written for reading and those chosen for speaking aloud. The length of sentences is key: spoken sentences are best short and smart.
7. William Hazlitt once said: 'An orator can hardly get beyond commonplaces: if he does, he gets beyond his hearers.' On the other hand, avoid clichés and jargon which throw an audience off key. Platitudes heaped upon clichés, as one gets at many a party political conference, are to be avoided.
8. Watch sensitive issues that can alarm, irritate or antagonise.
9. In reading a text or newspaper we can always glance back to remind ourselves of the argument. In a speech, signposts are needed to help the listeners remember. 'I would like to make three points. Firstly . . . etc' Avoid complex parenthetical clauses.

10. Avoid too many facts and figures. Details are difficult to remember. A speech is not a lecture.

11. Remember Aldous Huxley's advice: 'The nature of oratory is such that there has always been a tendency among politicians and clergyman to oversimplify complex matters. From a pulpit or a platform even the most conscientious of speakers finds it very difficult to tell the whole truth.'

12. Construct the memorable phrase, use powerful adjectives and don't be afraid of repetition. Find a punchy and telling conclusion. Get that off pat. A fluffed last sentence is a killer.

To summarise, a speech is not an essay. It has to be simpler, it has to be more pungent, the sentences have to be crisp and each has to tell its own story. Anything long and rambling ought to be broken up. When you have written it, read it out loud to make sure that the cadences and the structure flow properly. Audiences have a very short memory span, so keep the argument simple. Repeat to remind and, always, summarise at the end.

As Brian MacArthur has said, speeches are often ignored by history, either because there is no text available or because they read so much worse than they sound. They are generally only good or bad at the point of delivery. They look banal on the printed page. When read as literature, even the greatest can fail to impress. Nevertheless the duty of the speech-writer, be it the person making the speech themselves or a paid helper, is to write solely for

delivery. What makes a good 'historic' speech, as Peggy
Noonan realised, is also the heroic phrase. 'The wind of
change' or 'I have a dream', or 'Ask not what your country
can do for you, but what you can do for your country . . . '
are phrases that took on a life of their own, and reinforced
passionate beliefs in a convincing way.

While the speech-writer's art is often crucial, some of the
greatest speeches will still be those with no written text
whatsoever. The 'theatre' produced by a gifted speaker,
often without notes, is what will carry the day. Unless we
have that rare ability however, we need to work up a text, to
give the necessary quality to the language we intend to use.
Here the remarks of Sir Charles Powell, Private Secretary and
sometime speech-maker to Margaret Thatcher, reminiscing
in *The Times* (29 October, 1992), have a certain poignancy.

We learnt useful techniques. Never put anything worthwhile in the first draft, for it will be rejected. Keep the
structure for the second draft, for the first will inevitably
be condemned as not having one. Have the collected
works of Rudyard Kipling to hand. Don't even try to draft
a peroration until you are right up against a time limit,
because they are always revised right down to the line. Be
ready to stay up until six in the morning on the day of
delivery if necessary. But the satisfaction is immense . . .

# Body Language at the Podium

---

*Never make a gesture from the elbow –*
*that's a very weak gesture . . . If you make*
*it at all it must come from the shoulder*
*. . . The other great thing is that the*
*gesture must precede the phrase.*

Harold Macmillan,
British Prime Minister, recalling the
advice given to him by his predecessor,
David Lloyd George.

---

There are, essentially, eight rules of body language:

1. Smarten up. Men, adjust your tie before going on stage.
2. Make a 'stage' entry.
3. Stand upright but easily balanced. Try not to sway or rock.
4. Don't fiddle. Avoid distractions such as jangling money in your pockets, playing with your hair, your collar, or spectacles.
5. Watch your hands. Turn fiddles into gestures, using notes, or spectacles, if you have them for emphasis, raising them in your hand to make a point. A symbolic club movement can produce splendid emphasis.
6. Don't give the impression that you're hiding or sheltering behind the lectern. Men, if standing with no lectern between them and the audience, should avoid clasping their hands, as if protectively, in front of your flies.
7. Handle your notes precisely or discreetly. Don't shuffle.
8. Pause at the end, look round. Leave the stage with dignity.

# The Uses and Misuses of Humour

> *Once you get people laughing, they're listening and you can tell them almost anything.*
>
> Herbert Gerdner

Avoid putting on a funny man (or woman) act unless you are the one in a thousand who can. At a recent tourism awards dinner, the audience were totally repelled by the guest speaker regaling an audience with half an hour of dubious stand-up comedy. Again there are a few simple rules.

1. Don't if you can't. If you are bad at telling jokes, don't try.
2. If you are likely to fumble or mistime the punchline, forget it.
3. Don't take risks.
4. Avoid long stories or anecdotes, unless you are a good story-teller.
5. Make sure anything light-hearted fits in reasonably well with your theme. Don't mock others.
6. Stick to quick, apt one-liners, but rehearse well.
7. Never announce a joke in advance.
8. Don't ever apologise for a joke.
9. Make sure it is original. Old jokes kill. People may not remember the serious parts of your speech, but

they will remember if you've told them the joke before.

10. Don't be smutty unless you really know your audience. Ask: is it relevant? Is it acceptable? I remember being at a lunch given by a group of Newspaper Editors, where the Guest of Honour was the then Archbishop of Canterbury. He told a slightly risqué joke, which fell totally flat since these normally broad-minded journalists expected their Chief Prelate to set an example.

# Some Peculiarities of After-Dinner Speaking

*After-dinner speaking is the art of saying nothing, briefly.*

Edmund Fuller

Well, not quite, Mr Fuller. Even here there has to be a nub, a touch of substance amid the froth. But not too much, even if, as is often the case, the organisers or hosts have urged you to make it weighty. Major substance is not for that sort of occasion even if temperance is the order of the evening. In the rest of the animal kingdom, the tendency is to find a quiet piece of shade in which to go to sleep after food is killed and eaten. Human beings have not quite forgotten this urge and resent attempts, unless they are truly amusing, to keep them awake with indigestible moralising. Audience and speaker must know what each expects of the other. No surprises is the rule. Entertainment must come first, since after-dinner speaking is even more show-biz-linked than other sorts of public speaking, as is proved by the growing number of speakers agencies who will offer a range of fee-charging speakers for the annual 'do', from Selina Scott to David Frost, to Elton John, to Sir John Harvey-Jones. Take your pick. They have been carefully chosen because they can make the change lightly from the small screen or the concert platform or from the Board Room or AGM, without coming apart at the seams when faced with a live audience. They are all performers who need no pre-recording or retakes or tele-prompts to make them appear slick, attractive and amusing.

## The Big Set-Piece or Conference Speech

Any conference, party or cause-driven occasion will, in its aftermath, be classified by attendees as having 'come alive' or the reverse. One of the main reasons for a successful feel about such an occasion comes from the speeches of which it is largely composed. While speeches attempt to rally and to inspire, few succeed in exciting either passion or anything other than dutiful serious applause. A tiny number galvanise audiences into action, as the soldiers in Shakespeare's *Henry V* are inspired prior to the great battle. In my experience, of many party conferences, Michael Heseltine is one of the few, with all his singular policies and recent tactical mistakes set aside, who manages to barnstorm and hector and berate and inspire, and get away with it without being accused of being too much of a phoney.

While most people reading this book will not have to give a large set-piece speech to a huge audience, there is no harm in understanding something about what is required. If each sentence that you use has a life of its own, if you avoid fluffing things when you get to your feet, if you speak loudly and with conviction, if you avoid long and complex interwoven attempts at serious argument, you will achieve a great deal. Even more than normal, your effort must not be so much with content as with delivery. The people out there want to be cheered and exhorted: if both can be achieved, you have succeeded. But it has to be done with care otherwise it does not work – as Matthew Parris, writing in *The Times* (8 October, 1992) found when he was exposed to the then Home Secretary, Kenneth Clarke's, efforts:

The Home Secretary had hoped to quicken pulses: but how far can you get with declarations like, 'Community sentences will be the sort which have an effect!' We await a Home Secretary who dares promise community sentences which don't. Mr Clarke then tried to rouse himself to indignation during a passage on the 'the problems posed by new age travellers and ravers' but, puffed cheeks and shiny features emerging from a striped shirt strobing in the TV lights, plus tie with psychedelic swirls, Mr Clarke looked more like a middle-aged dad trying to be a raver, than their persecutor.

Mr Parris, at his best, ended up thus.

Mr Clarke can punch the air all he pleases but, though he looks like a bruiser, he's actually a thinker, and representatives are not fooled. They don't want a thinker. He was rewarded with a crouching ovation.

## The Few Informal Words

---

*It takes more than three weeks to prepare a good impromptu speech.*

Mark Twain

---

If you are required to make a few casual remarks, this requires thinking about just as much as any major speech. You can, with a few words, make an effect with some quick and light turn of phrase that might not stand up to scrutiny in front of a large and hungry audience, but a farewell speech to someone leaving the office, a brief vote of thanks, a few words at a friendly dinner party, should be well prepared in advance even though you intend to be on your feet for less than a minute. Short must mean pithy and to the point. You have no time to be eloquent. Then sit down.

# Training

*All the great speakers were bad speakers at first.*

Ralph Waldo Emerson

You, like Mr Hustle, Mr Grey and Mr Wright, can learn to improve. If you are going to have to do a lot of public speaking, reading what is written here, followed by one single day's session with an experienced tutor, may be enough to remove a blockage, to disperse most nerves, and to set you up for life. Like riding a bicycle, once learned, public speaking skills stay with you. My approach is to get my clients to make a short, pre-prepared speech, at most only two or three minutes long, and then gradually, after analysing their performance on the monitor screen, to have them polish it and their presence, presentation and paralanguage – the whole package – again and again, until they develop a smooth, seamless, and convincing performance. It really does work. Try it.

## Autocues

If you need them, well, you need them. Some autocues are very sophisticated, but they will, unless you handle them well, give away that you are merely reading your lines. A real speech has hesitations and spontaneity. Robin Day has argued (in his autobiography) that only Ronald Reagan could use one well, but then he was a professional actor. To quote Day (and his book is well worth reading on this and on many other 'personal impact' subjects): 'For someone trying to persuade, or amuse, or inspire their audience, as a politician or public figure may wish to do, then the use of autocue is liable to kill personality, sincerity and spontaneity . . . I have never seen or heard a rip-roaring, passionate, witty or inspiring platform speech delivered from autocue.'

# Audio/Visual Aids

I make no attempt here to cover what is a well-discussed subject, beyond saying that a speech or a lecture should never debase itself by being an adjunct to, or the mere narration of, a slide show. As I write, I am still recovering from last night where the speaker at an awards ceremony merely read out the text of each slide he screened. We read them quicker than he could read them out. He spoke for half an hour. Boredom set in after two minutes. A visual aide/slide or whatever should be that and that alone, a back-up to the real message. The same goes for blackboards, whiteboards, flip charts and film. And get them in the right order, the right way up. There is no excuse for a sloppy audio/visual presentation.

# Question and Answer Sessions

---

*Let your speech be always with grace,*
*seasoned with salt, that ye may know how*
*ye ought to answer every man.*

Bible: Colossians

---

There are no hard and fast rules about how to deal with the question and answer sessions which often follow a speech. It is, however, a good idea for the Chairman of the session, (or you yourself) to repeat the question. It helps the audience, particularly if the questioner was difficult to hear in a large room or hall, and it also gives you time to think. Even the silliest questions should be treated with great patience and courtesy. The audience may laugh at a naive questioner: you should not.

# Hostile Audiences

Most audiences are inclined to be kind at least at the beginning of the speech. You will never get the reverence which is afforded to the Queen or a company chairman or someone set in authority over those who are listening. But providing you follow the rules and do not insult or bore people, you will go a long way before you start being heckled. It may be, of course, that you are already known for some extreme view, or the audience consists of 500 angry mill workers whom you are about to sack, in which case you may have an uphill struggle.

Here the five basic rules are:

1. If you can't cope, don't try.
2. Never lose your temper. React with equanimity even if provoked.

3. Try to get the majority on your side.
4. Don't let the occasion degenerate into a slanging match.
5. Volunteer to discuss issues privately with persistent hecklers later.

Heckling is something that the skilled speaker can use to his or her advantage. At the 1992 Tory Party Conference some journalists felt that Michael Heseltine's retort to hecklers was so good that it might even have been pre-planned. He certainly used one of the oldest tricks of the trade by handing the Euro sceptics a bait. It went like this.

'The whole history of the European Community has been to advance by centralisation in Brussels,' he suggested. A cry of, 'It shouldn't' predictably filled the pause he deliberately left. Mr Heseltine responded forcefully. 'Then what the heck are you complaining about when John Major has reversed the process?' As cheers outweighed protests, Mr Heseltine added sarcastically: 'This voice of the Tory party. I cannot understand a word it says and, even if I did, it is not worth listening to.' A lone heckler refused to back down. Heseltine delivered the knock-out punch. 'One against so many. You just lost.'

# Simultaneous/Consecutive Interpretation

A brief word here about speeches, or interviews or any presentation where translation into another language is necessary. The best is, of course, simultaneous interpretation where the translator is sitting in a sound-proof box, and, as you speak, puts it into the other language with instant fluency for the benefit of an audience listening to you through earphones. In less structured settings, where the technology is lacking, consecutive interpretation becomes necessary. Here you have to speak in pre-agreed soundbites – not too short, not too long and then you have to pause while the interpretation is made. Your speech will consequently last twice as long. Inevitably, the impetus and impact of any such speech is lost in the delivery. The emphasis and drama, unless the interpreter is a particularly good actor, will disappear, and the attention of your audience is bound to flag during the periods when they are listening, without comprehension, while you deliver your message in English. You cannot expect the interpreter to translate your paralanguage and your body language, and that too weakens the overall effect. The solution is, therefore, only to use this latter when nothing better is available, and if it is pure fact and argument that you wish to convey, as, say, at a sales promotion event. You will seldom convince on a more evocative subject. You will never quite be able to judge what impact you are making on a foreign audience. Jokes, in particular, translate badly. When I joined the British Diplomatic service many years ago, our instructions in a rather pompous guide to etiquette were, 'beware the dangers of wit and the pitfalls of humour, particularly when dealing with foreigners.' The same still applies today, not least because humour can be misunderstood and can even cause offence.

# The Ending

> *Follow the advice I was given when singing in supper clubs: 'Get off while you're ahead; always leave them wanting more.' Make sure you have finished speaking before your audience has finished listening. A talk, as Mrs Hubert Humphrey reminded her husband, need not be eternal to be immortal.*
>
> Dorothy Sarnoff

> *A speech is like a love affair. Any fool can start it but to end it requires considerable skill.*
>
> Lord Mancroft

Conclusions are an important part of every speech. They are especially welcome when they come close to the beginning. David Wright remembers the dictum about conclusions, namely that you tell them what you have told them and then make sure they know that you have come to the end. John Hustle, by contrast, never seems to end, and, each time the audience sits on the edge of their chairs waiting for him to do so, he finds a new lease of life, while Andy Grey suddenly is not there. He has ended what he wanted to say without giving his audience any clue, by way of a finale, that his task is over.

There are two little words which always catch the attention of the most apathetic audience. These are: 'In conclusion . . . ' Some speakers seem to get a second wind from then on. Make sure your aftermath of this is very brief indeed. My final piece of advice is to memorise that final sentence and make it upbeat and punchy. Fluffing the last line can kill the lot.

# SECTION FIVE

# Career Interview Skills

> *There may be other reasons for a man's not speaking in public than want of resolution; he may have nothing to say . . . The happiest conversation is that of which nothing is distinctly remembered, but a general effect of pleasing impression.*
>
> Samuel Johnson

> *Talking and eloquence are not the same: to speak, and to speak well, are two things.*
>
> Ben Jonson

As I said at the beginning of this book, when three candidates for a top job, all with equally promising CVs, all with equal background experience, are being interviewed, the one that communicates best will, other things being equal, come out on top. David Wright knows this and has prepared his responses with great care. The other two, Hustle and Grey, are by now generally aware of this too, but Hustle still feels he will get through as he has always done in the past, by parading his patter in a non-stop flow. Alan Grey, by contrast, knows what he wants to say, but takes a long time getting around to saying it, by which time the interviewers have lost patience: they cut him short and get on to the next question before he has answered the first. It would have been so easy for him to rehearse short and clear answers to such common basic questions as Why do you want the job? Why do you think you would be good at it? and Why are you leaving your present job? without coming out with a long and incoherent version of his past history and philosophy of life. Careers are made or broken on the back of a few ill-chosen or well-thought out words. Empathy soothes one's reception. The development of interview skills is important in delivering any message. The same basic guidelines apply to all kinds of interview, whether career orientated, or conducted in public, or with the media, or in a group session.

By and large, in the day-to-day running of our lives, we get by with only adequate social skills. But these are seldom enough to make a significant impact during a tense and sometimes very brief job or promotion interview. No matter how good our thoughts and ambitions are, they are worthless unless we can communicate them effectively and immediately to others within the *time allowed*. We need to cut out any needless or boring information. We have to get ourselves straight away onto the same wavelength as those sitting across the table. Life is too short and too competitive to interview badly. We can learn in many different ways but there is nothing to beat training and watching the experience of others. Look around at colleagues and friends. How would you advise them to improve? Then draw the lessons for yourself.

Looking, for a moment, at the career interview from the point of view of the interviewer, if the latter is experienced, they will know to suppress some of the prejudices we discussed earlier to which they and we all are subject. It is all too easy to pick up a CV and from that to make certain prejudgements that are quite possibly totally wrong, just as, in everyday life, we may consider that all Germans must be efficient, all Italians make good lovers, or that all old Etonians are aristocratic. CVs are never enough. Indeed for the very top posts they are taken for granted. When you are up for the job of Chairman, how many 'O' Levels you once obtained, or even what degree you have, tends to have little or no relevance. When an interviewer comes face to face with the interviewee they may have to force themselves to put aside certain prejudices and weed out irrelevant detail from important fact. But still the primacy rule, as we have seen, tends to outweigh reality. People only see what they want to see, which is why, once again, first impressions assume such enormous importance. Studies have long shown that managers in industry and commerce are well known to appoint to key positions people 'like' or agreeable to themselves, even if they are not quite 'clones'. We all react to people on the basis of 'similar' experiences of 'similar' types in the past, relating them to our present needs, expectations and interests. Our 'perceptual grasp' of individuals can be very different from their reality.

At any moment we are, after all, aware of millions of things around us, but we only select a very few items on which to base a decision or a course of action. That is the reason why we have such very little time in an interview to make people like us or want to employ us. As somebody once said, we have to be like flower arrangers, putting the best blooms to the front and keeping the wilting ones out of sight. This leads back to the need to dress for the occasion. No matter how good your CV, if you come in dressed like a down-and-out or in some weird get up like a leather-clad biker, or with no tie, or with a ring through your nose, though it may show prejudice, few are going to believe that you have reasonable potential on offer.

Continuing on this neo-psychological theme, as a general rule, our attention in life tends to be drawn towards stimuli that are large rather than small, bright rather than dull, loud rather than quiet, strong rather than weak, standing out rather than merged with their surroundings. Designers of road signs employ similar factors to attract and hold people's attention. Hazard warning signs tend to be flashing and bright rather than dull and static, to alert the attention of motorists. Advertisers on television often set their products into unusual surroundings to attract the attention of the consumers. We need not go to the extent of those who always present their vehicles driving across impossible terrain, up mountains, through burning fields, or triumphantly manoeuvering through avalanches, on routes that none of us would ever dare to drive on. But we do, in how we dress and present ourselves, have to operate within a framework that means something to those whom we intend to impress.

In career interviews, from both sides of the table, we make judgements about those across from us that are influenced by tiny features of dress, colour, speech. That first, dangerously brief, impression may eventually turn out to be irrelevant to the assessment we want to make but if someone slouches in their chair, or mumbles, or wears an entirely inappropriate tie, or if a woman wears too much of a plunging neckline or a too short a skirt, emotions, both favourable and unfavourable, are bound to affect the cooler judgements of those who are trying to make the selection. This may be wrong: this may lead to idiotic decisions over appointing or not appointing; but these are the facts of life.

We have also found that we discriminate in favour of characteristics the other person has in common with us. We may think we are immune but if we see in someone else a trait that is shared by us, or if we see characteristics or looks or habits or background that are common to people we like or love, such as members of our family or close friends, then the stranger sitting in front of us will, rightly or wrongly, be imbued with other favourable characteristics which we assume they have, even though there is no other evidence for such a belief. Even if Mr Hustle is a much more sober and thoughtful person than he appears, the fact that he is always in natty gent's suits with over polished shoes and a rather too flamboyant tie, will count against him because he looks so much like a television spiv, or the used car salesman at the garage round the corner. Equally, Alan Grey has a great deal to offer, but never gets beyond go because his slip-shod appearance, unpressed suit and tired tie and shirt, reminds his inter-viewers of some latter-day down and out.

# Pre-Interview Preparation:

Getting down to the detail of pre-interview preparation, there are a number of points to consider.

1. Who will interview you: an individual or a panel? What can you find out about them, their interests and likely prejudices?
2. What do you want out of the interview? What exactly is the job/position? Research it as much as you can.
3. What are they looking for in terms of skills and experience?
4. What good qualities do you want to project and want them to notice?
5. How can you downplay/avoid revealing your less good qualities: the flipside factor?
6. What should you wear for best effect. Always avoid extremes of dress.

7. Ask yourself: Why should they listen to me? Why should they want me?

8. Remember the fifteen-second rule.

9. Don't talk too much.

10. Rehearse certain answers in advance. There are many standard questions: Why do you want the job? How much do you know about it? Why do you think you would suit? Is the money factor a major consideration? These always come up and can be carefully thought out before almost any type of interview.

11. Work out your key message: in most interviews you have time to put across a maximum of three points.

12. Prepare yourself for the unexpected question by having a formula on the lines set out in the next section. A powerful *response* rather than the precise *answer* is often the key.

# The Interview Itself

---

When people are least sure, they are often most dogmatic.

J.K. Galbraith

---

Marshall Mcluhan argued in *The Medium is the Message* that message and manner are inextricably linked. Perform well and your message gets through. And, as Eliza Doolittle discovered, a certain amount of training helps, to ensure that, whatever your background and accent, your diction comes across clearly, and is fully understandable.

You must prepare to go into the interview with the clear aim of giving off attractive stimuli, and ensuring that your body language and your paralanguage matches, or lives up to, your actual words. That may seem a tall order, imprecisely defined, but you can achieve this by creating the right balance of assertiveness and impact that projects your personal competence, and by being clear without overstating your case. Here are ten pointers.

1. Enter the room confidently. Try a smile.
2. Sit up. Unless you are effortlessly superior, look alert.
3. Look at who is asking the questions. Too much eye movement can make you look shifty.
4. Watch your hand movements. Avoid gestures that distract attention or suggest excessive nervousness.
5. Speak clearly.
6. Watch your time: it's short. On the other hand, as in speech-making, a carefully timed pause can catch the interviewer's attention.
7. Say what *you* want to say. *You know more about what you are going to say than they do.*
8. Don't bring in any notes. In general they do not work in interviews.
9. Be positive, enthusiastic, but not pushy.
10. Don't ramble. Keep it tight.

Let me end on a highly controversial note. Whether you think it abhorrent or not, for a large number of good people, particularly in certain professions and institutions such as the City, in the Armed Forces, and indeed in politics (where party selection committees are notorious) the spouse factor is increasingly important. I know of one potential headmaster who failed to get a job at a public school because his wife was perceived by the governors as not being up to the task which, it has to be accepted, is an important one at a boarding school. Equally, someone coming up to be Colonel of the Regiment was marked down and eventually lost out because his wife was seen to be a handicap in the job he was meant to do. In politics, many is the case of outstanding or adequate candidates, both male and female, who might have made it on their own and become MPs, but, as the result of a less than useful spouse, and spouses are always recognised as an integral part of the election package in terms of winning votes, have failed to get selected. Remember, if you are going for a job when you know your partner's qualities are going to be assessed as part and parcel of the process, then it is up to you (and your partner) to make sure that *both of you* take heed of the points made in this book. If that is objectionable to you, try for a job where the spouse does not count.

# SECTION SIX

# Media Interview Skills

*When ideas fail, words come in very handy.*

Goethe

*He knew the precise psychological moment when to say nothing.*

Oscar Wilde – *Dorian Gray*

*Something's going awry here. I mean, if I just listen to the question, I can answer whatever it is. But if I think it's going to be on [the script], I don't listen to the question, I just look at [the script].*

George Bush, complaining over an open microphone that supposedly spontaneous questions from a teachers' group were not coming in the order his staff had prepared for him.

*You can't run a country by sound-bite.*

John Major

Maybe not, Mr Major. But, along with your visual impact, you can be elected by them. That *Sound-Vision-Bite*, is what wins the day. I believed, for a short time, that the

Conservatives were bound to lose the 1992 election. Three days before it, on the 6th April, John Major was interviewed live on Panorama by David Dimbleby. It was a tough interview with tough questions, which, in purely verbal terms, the Prime Minister in his best 'earnest camel' way, answered well. But in visual terms, the programme was stacked against him. Deliberate or not, the camera shots and angles seemed unbelievably biased. Dimbleby was shown large; Major, shrunk by the cameras, appeared insignificant, like a small boy facing a headmaster who had just caught him as he emerged, blinking, into the daylight, after smoking behind the gymnasium. At best, it was megapundit interrogating minor mandarin, the latter insisting on speaking his own brand of officialese. Major's appearance (and he is gradually improving) with his glued-on hairstyle and his strangulated or 'trapped' voice (note how he pronounces 'want' as *'wunt'*) showed him up for what he was: a decent man in spectacles. But not the stuff of heroes, or national leaders. Neil Kinnock, however, slave of his image gurus, got it still worse, and snatched defeat from the jaws of victory. Dressed to look like a statesman, complete with red rose, hands clenched in front of him to demonstrate calm as opposed to the controlled aggression which his normal finger-jabbing style of debate demonstrates, he ended up looking like a puppet dressed up to look like a statesman. Meanwhile, the boundless sea of his sentences, constantly demonstrating that while he had the power of speech he had little power of communication, poured out unabated, till the majority saw no other choice.

These two scenes illustrate Peter Jenkins' remark that 'politics is television' – in other words, that the media molds the message in most matters of public concern.

The gnashing of sound-bites has been the principal language of electioneering for several decades past, just as great oratory helped win seats in centuries long gone. Aneurin Bevan may have complained that Churchill's 'mediocrity of his thinking is concealed by the majesty of his language', but it proved to be a formidable bit of window dressing during the Second World War. Nowadays, the mass media would have emasculated his impassioned verbiage, a short clip would have been screened, a fragment of a sentence appearing in print, and the rest would be left on the cutting room floor. As the veteran American political commentator, George Will, pointed out recently: 'When George Bush wants to say that he will not raise taxes, he announces: "Read my lips, no new taxes." You cannot imagine Lincoln saying, "Read my lips, no slaves." That's not the way people used to talk in this country.'

For most of us, including Messrs Hustle, Grey and Wright, when we are being interviewed by the media, it is not only against each other that we are competing, but against comparisons with the professionals from television and elsewhere. Those on the outside looking at you, your audience, inevitably compare your performance with other ones that they have seen on television that night. Television is a high-powered medium. It demands the best. You have to prepare well before appearing on it.

The media, and particularly television, amplifies everything. Impressions rather than details prevail. Perversely, television also creates a strange intimacy between subject and viewer, and, consequently, some of those who appear in front of the cameras are actually shrunk by the TV lights and the small screen. Try watching some public figure on your set with the sound turned right down. As I suggested you do when you are training yourself in public speaking, judge how much they really impress. The voice, the presence, the overall image, the 'vision-bite' is somehow put under a microscope by television and strengths as well as defects are exaggerated before the viewing public. It is a great levelling process; small people can be made to look grand and impressive by means of a good media-related performance. By contrast, competent people can be deflated and even destroyed. Television, after all, effectively ruined the former Prime Minister Alec Douglas Home, who always appeared wooden and unhappy on the small screen. How much more might he suffer now when media interviewers are getting increasingly abrasive. Today there is even less automatic respect for authority, less public belief that the truth is being spoken simply because some senior person says it is the case.

To take another example from political life, the European Commissioner, Sir Leon Brittan, does himself no justice when he goes on television. He is a victim of the small screen and appears to look superciliously down his nose at his fireside audience. By contrast, in the flesh he is amusing, clever and articulate, one of the few outstandingly intelligent men in political life today. He holds a live audience with ease; each of his sentences flows effortlessly, if undramatically, into the next, in a constant stream of thought. One reason why his delivery style translates badly to television is because he puts a standard, repetitive stress on what he says, each third or fourth word being given the same push or thrust, again and again and again. Yet at close quarters his mind shows through. How many of his colleagues can speak on a complex subject for up to forty minutes, without benefit of notes, let alone a text?

David Wright has now learned that, in public speaking, while he can have a text of his speech to hand, he is much better using cue cards. John Hustle has also learned to work from a text as a device to keep his flow of patter under control. He has at last realised that self-discipline is more important than reams of words. Alan Grey needs his text too; it is still too much of a support, but he has been prevailed upon to rehearse again and again, and he has adopted a style of highlighting, with a yellow highlighter, some of his key phrases, which gives an easier flow. He has also developed a useful practice of making 'cue' notes with a felt-tip pen at the side of his text to remind him to keep looking up at the audience rather than down at the papers in front of him. Watching his own progress on a television monitor has increased his self-confidence. He not only knows his subject but realises that he can let go the crutch of reading his full text without falling over.

But texts and cue cards are of no use in media interviews. So how can you prepare? One such trick of the trade is to draw up and practise from a list of 'bullet-points' which you want to make. But before all that, you need to realise that when you come to be interviewed, no matter how important you may think what you have to say is, the news editor is king. Or, rather, time is king. In any given day there is a 'news hole', only just so much that can be fitted into a newscast or report. Much depends on how much other 'news' is around. A 'good' day for news – an earthquake or a train crash – may wipe your most statesmanlike speech or interview into oblivion. Even fairly substantial news items on television last no more than ninety seconds, and what normally would be a fairly significant issue can be ignored or pushed aside by the instant demands of a bomb outrage or a royal divorce. In consequence, it is only the most relevant remark, the one that is pertinent, or timely, or amusing, or *apropos*, or suits the editor's instant thinking, that survives. The words of the wise and the foolish are equally cut down to size. But the important thing to remember is that, if TV commercials can make a telling point in under half a minute, so can you, though when it comes to political sound-bites, one cynic, CBS Evening News executive producer, Erik Sorensen, speaking about the network's new policy of airing only campaign sound-bites that were longer than thirty seconds, remarked wryly: 'Frankly, we're sceptical whether we can keep it up. It's very hard to find them (ie. politicians) saying anything substantive for as long as thirty seconds.'

Around 1968 in the United States, when television journalists started using the term 'sound-bite', a Presidential candidate was allowed to speak for up to forty-three seconds, uninterrupted by comment or commercial. Brevity already ruled. In fact any speech (Gladstone spoke for four and three quarter hours in the 1888 Budget debate) is now edited down to an average of an eight point five seconds sound-bite if it is going out on US television, and a slightly more generous average of sixteen seconds, if you were campaigning to be a British Prime Minister in the 1992 Election. How much shorter can they get? Because of this constraint on time, brevity is something that has become rather more marked, and welcome, following the televising of the British House of Commons. The former Speaker of the House, Sir Bernard Wetherall, noted a steady progression towards shorter sentences in debates, as his fellow Parliamentarians realised that long sentences, like long speeches, (what Americans sometimes refer to as stem-winders) got axed out of existence.

In media interviews, too, you have a very brief time indeed to say what you want. You may have a lot of important political or business information to impart, so getting it effectively transmitted to a wider audience is crucial. Although concerned mainly with media interviews – largely on radio and television – much of what follows also applies to newspaper interviews. Anyone in any position of prominence has now got to learn how to project succinctly. And it is not just a matter of choosing the right words. Style is as important in speech-making, and media training is crucial to any would-be successful executive. It is a relatively easy skill to improve on in comparison with other qualifications we have to study for in the course of our careers, yet it still gets ignored even by top managers. There are increasingly specialised types of interview techniques to be met as well, such as learning how to deal with face-to-face sessions, discussion groups and being interviewed 'down the line', where the interviewer is not in the same location as the interviewee. A little time practising the necessary skills pays instant and major dividends.

If you expect, in some new career spot, that you are going to have to spend any time at all in television studios, or even if you only want to be prepared for such an eventuality, the more opportunities you have of getting used to the glare of the arc lights, the need to be made-up before going on and of not being distracted by the many monitor screens with which you are faced or the tele-prompt system which your interlocutor has, the better. Admittedly, no matter how much training he has, the strains and stresses of being in a television studio will probably mean that Alan Grey will never be totally happy there, but he will, with guidance, make not too bad an impression. David Wright, if he learns to keep his eyes on the interviewer rather than letting them wander round the studio which gives him a slightly shifty-eyed look, will do passably well, but here, John Hustle may, in certain circumstances, actually come across the best, because television audiences are, after all, conditioned to listen to a lot of glib patter at the best of times.

A lot of the technique is not difficult at all. Little things, like knowing that someone may suddenly emerge out of the darkness and give a dust of powder to your forehead if it is pouring with sweat, or that they are unexpectedly going to stick a hand up your shirt to adjust the lead on a buttonhole microphone, or that there is to be a commercial break without any warning, are all part and parcel of the same learning process. If you are going straight on live, tips about straightening your tie and making sure your jacket is not hunched up over your neck and so on are easy to forget.

Once again, a short check-list is helpful. Prior to the interview:

1. Find out who is the interviewer. What is their style? Is he or she the fact-seeking or the point-scoring type?
2. Watch videos, if you can, of their interview style. Even habitual interviewees can be thrown by an unexpected approach as a result either of deviousness or, more usually, because the interviewer, or the producer, thinks it makes for better television viewing.

3. Who else is being interviewed? Who are you being
   matched up with?
4. Identify what you want to get out of it.
5. What do they want out of it? What are the dangers?
   Are they likely to trap you with some tricky or
   embarrassing questions?
6. Don't try to memorise answers. But have a mental list
   of your key bullet points.

Developing the first two points listed above – it is essential
to know whether your interrogator models him or herself
on the aggressive Walden-style of interviewing, where the
interviewer seems more intent on making a name for
himself, in producing a clash rather than eliciting information. I contrast Walden with the more expantional Sir
Robin Day, who can be aggressive and tough, but at the
same time takes some heed of the response. Other interviewers come into the category of the Dimbleby brothers –
thoughtful, pungent, but in the end courteous, or follow
the mocking and cynical Jeremy Paxman mode. To my
mind, especially for the longer type of interview, the
David Frost style, where the interviewee is lead, cleverly
and cunningly, but then allowed to say his or her part
without undue interruption, is best. The veteran American
broadcaster, Walter Cronkite, always said that David
Frost's interview style was the best on British television:
leading, goading, eliciting, but not an approach that is
over-burdened with the Frost presence. All these 'style'

interviewers are again very different from, say, Sue Lawley on *Desert Island Discs*. This technique is designed to encourage reminiscence, and can be used to brilliant effect by an expert, someone like Dr Anthony Clare, who in his radio series, *In The Psychiatrist's Chair*, is interested in getting the patient to keep talking, even to ramble, thus ultimately revealing all.

## Dos and Don'ts in the Studio

*His socks compelled one's attention without losing one's respect.*

Saki

If you have an opportunity to familiarise yourself, you will find that radio studios tend to be small, sound-proofed boxes, with a green baize or sound absorbent table upon which are placed several microphones. The control room operators monitor events from beyond a sound-proof glass screen. The producer will probably want you to try your voice for level unless you are going straight on live. It is a sensible practice to make sure that you do not have coins or anything rattling in your pockets, or papers that are going to rustle too much and distract the listeners' attention. Occasionally you may be interviewed down the line for radio and have to go alone into a little box and put headphones on. By and large you will be guided from then on as to what you should do, though being all on your own, talking to a disembodied voice somewhere miles away, can be a bit disconcerting at first.

Television studios can range from a small set to a huge studio. Again, if you can view what you are going to be faced with before the event, then all to the good. Little things can throw you as much as major ones. I remember being on the Wogan Show and finding it peculiar that, while I could hear the studio audience, I could not see them because of the way the set was adjusted, and I had to judge reaction by sound alone, in terms of applause or the reverse. My own most telling reaction, and I suspect that of most other people, tends to be to the intensity of the lights in a television studio, both in terms of the glare and, more importantly, the heat that is generated which causes sweating even in the coolest victim. Thus the necessity for the constant attentions of make-up teams who are ready with a dust of powder to mop up the rivulets of sweat that shine in a highly unprepossessing way if not speedily disguised.

Remember:

1. Accept pre-make-up if it is offered. It is perfectly masculine – indeed many men need it more.

Blotchiness, or red noses, or spots, are bad for your message and your image.

2. Choose as stable and upright a chair as possible. (You may have no choice.)

3. Lean forward a little, square on to the camera. A tucked-in chin suggests defensiveness, so keep it up.

4. Never slouch, no matter how comfortable the chair. Crossed legs are better on women than men.

5. Look authoritative. You are master of your material. With practice you can actually control the interview 'agenda'.

6. Prepare your mental sound-bites. Beware, on the other hand, of one-word answers, which usually sound too curt or rude. Keep it simple. Life is full of people saying bland unmemorable things. Work up a few punch lines and have them ready to deliver. Get in with the last word.

7. Always look at the interviewer or whoever is talking. Unless you are expert at it, do not look at the camera. You should normally only look at the lens if you are being interviewed down the line, or being doorstepped in the street.

8. Watch your body language. Don't allow your eyes to wander to the left or the right or you will appear shifty. As always, good eyelock is essential. No sly looks at the monitor screen. Looking upwards tends, on the small screen, to convey an impression that you are seeking divine inspiration.

9. Don't fiddle. Bored cameramen love to focus on restless movements or nervous gestures, foot tapping, or (with men) clasped hands over flies.

10. Pull your dress or jacket well down at the back or else you will look hunched, as if you have no neck. Men should sit on the tails of their jackets. Watch straining shirt buttons over a paunch, hairy gaps between (male) trouser bottoms and tops of socks, and squint ties. Women: do not wear too much make-up or plunging necklines (which can plunge even further if weighted by a button mike) or flashy jewellery. All these can be distracting.

Remember, once again, *that you know more about what you want to say than the interviewer does*. You must make sure you say it, despite what they try to make you say. The tighter you say your piece the better and the less chance there is of it being edited down. Matthew Arnold talked about those who were 'never bound by the despotism of fact'. You always have to be, though you can sometimes get away with being a fraction economical with the truth. If they keep to the above, our three candidates, Wright, Hustle and Grey, will go away from the interview at least confident that they have made their point. They may not have done it with total panache or fluency, but they will have held the ring, particularly if they keep their contributions clipped to the best performance length.

# The TV Interview at Home,
# in the Office or in the Street

The trouble about interviews away from the studio is that, quite often, they come up unexpectedly. I can remember, when I was working at Buckingham Palace, suddenly being confronted by three television crews and a host of photographers and journalists as I rather absentmindedly opened my front door, ready to take my two young children on their morning run to school. My thoughts were on scarves and school books and whether I had enough petrol in the car, not on what the press that morning thought I ought to be commenting on. My children later complained that I had been rather rude to these nice people who had got up early to greet and talk to me: being abrupt does little good either. You may feel that in front of your own house or outside your office, you will be more in control. It is an easy assumption to fall into: these settings are just as difficult, just as tricky, just as full of elephant traps as more formal locations. As a general rule, therefore, do not give interviews when you are door-stepped. It always looked rushed. It always appears as if you are talking under a certain amount of duress. Tell the media, quietly and firmly, that you will talk to them in your own time, and when you are ready and prepared. Let them wait, or come back in half an hour when you have your hair combed, your tie straight, and are not surrounded by children who are anxious to get to school on time.

# Twelve Bewares

*People don't seem to realise that it takes time and effort and preparation to think. Politicians are far too busy talking to think.*

Bertrand Russell

Beware the following:

1. Being quoted out of context. Make your point concisely.
2. Being edited down. Never give them enough to do so. They have to use it all or nothing.
3. Being out of date. Make sure you know when you are being screened or the interview is to be broadcast.
4. The human interest story that will beat your most reasonable argument. (The sacked worker may have been dishonest, but if he is filmed, out of work, with a worried wife and two sweet children by his side, you've lost.)
5. Being interviewed down the line. It's never so authoritative.

6. Being sidetracked on to some separate issue.
7. Being caught off guard. Agree, as I said before, to be interviewed in *your* time.
8. The same question being put different ways.
9. The 'we already know x from y and are just looking for confirmation' trap.
10. The negative question. 'Do you not agree that . . . '
11. Having words put in your mouth.
12. Alcohol. There is no such thing as alcohol-induced Dutch courage. Experienced cameramen can tell by your colouring if you have had even one drink.

# Dealing with Tricky Questions

Reason is dull. Emotion is interesting. Interviewers think of themselves as the devil's advocates – but they are also there to be used by you. And audiences are enormously fickle, with low tolerance levels and attention spans. When some (particularly politicians) answer a question, few who hear it will actually listen. If they do, they will seldom remember. To say something memorable you really have to work at it.

The *Turnaround* or *Turnabout* is an increasingly common way of manipulating or avoiding a difficult question or getting your own points across. While some interviewers are skilled at bringing you back to what they are actually asking, for most of the time the clever interviewee will get away with it, particularly if the interviewer is also of the breed that does not actually listen to answers, so busy are they preparing the next question. At its most simple, the Turnaround takes the following form. Whatever the question, the interviewee responds by saying,

- I think the question you are trying to ask is . . .
- The question you should be asking is . . .
- Before I answer that, let me just say . . .
- You are getting away from the real point which is that . . .
- You're right there, but let me add . . .
- I would put it another way . . .
- That may be true, but another thing I am certain about is . . .
- I thought I'd covered that, but I'll say that again . . .
- That's not the real issue . . . (This implies the interviewer has got it all wrong or gone off on the wrong tack.)
- You may thing that's what we're getting at, but . . .
- I'm glad you asked that question . . . (You're not, but appearing to approve of the question helps.) You then answer your own question.
- Another version of this is: 'That's a very interesting question, but . . .' Or, quite simply, 'You've got it all wrong.'

–   Watch out for 'Now let me make myself entirely
    clear . . . ' (Oh yes?) Or 'Far be it from me to . . . '
    (which means the reverse).

This Turnaround technique, which is sometimes known as
bridging, confronts the interviewer with a difficult decision: to let it ride and have you win, or to return and press
the point firmly and get accused of being hostile. That's
their problem. *Your technique is to be ready with responses
rather than mere answers to the questions asked.*

If you think all the above is far-fetched, it is worth
recalling that a recent study at York University (Peter Bull
and Kate Mayer) found that Mrs Thatcher and Mr Kinnock
between them used something like thirty different ways of
*not answering* the question they were asked in interviews. It
is a great skill. Sir Robin Day got so infuriated by the then
Prime Minister's ability to avoid what she was being
asked, that one day he is said to have exploded: 'And
what is your answer to my first question, Mrs Thatcher?'
She was the first to realise that many interviews only make
news when there is a gaffe. She set the agenda. Usually she
won.

To end on an optimistic note, by and large, my experience of training leaders and managers in political, business
and public life generally (and John Hustle, Alan Grey and
David Wright, who will keep their separate styles and
approach will prove this point in their different ways), is
that they will always be better in interviews, in the cut and

thrust of cross-questioning, than in the more formal setting of making a public speech. The reason for this is simple. The latter is contrived; the former is much more like real life, the daily debate and argument which takes place across the boardroom tables of life. The adrenalin pumps faster when directly challenged.

# SECTION SEVEN

# A Final Word

> *I've been asked to speak to you. You've been asked to listen to me. If you finish before me . . .*
>
> Michael Sinclair

> *Delivery, delivery, delivery*
>
> Demosthenese

Some people have a natural gift of making people listen. Others open their mouths and are an immediate switch-off like the speaker who asked his audience if everyone could hear him, to which the cynical heckle was 'I can, but I'll gladly swap with someone who can't.' Equally, some are born with an innate grace or charm. Others lack any trace of it. Reagan had it; Nixon did not; but who was the more able? Edward Heath had none; John Major has it (and it can be a dangerous commodity if ill-used) as a helpful back-up where more effective leadership qualities are perhaps lacking.

Whatever you have been born with, improving your impact, your delivery, your presence and your paralanguage, should take the highest place in your personal agenda, not just for selfish, self-promotional reasons, but because if you project well in whatever you do you will win out over an opposition that does not, both for yourself and for the organisations that you lead or represent. I asked at the beginning of this book, why do more people not learn to communicate more effectively and why are we not taught this discipline just as much as we are other skills? Particularly in this age of mass communication, it is absurd to ignore such an important ability, which can make all the difference between success and failure in any career. The most critical thing, which John Hustle, Alan Grey and David Wright have now learnt, is that the skills set out in this book can make the difference between success and a life of missed opportunities. They have been prompted by colleagues, by friends, by circumstance, and particularly by seeing how they appear via the television monitor, to work on their personal impact skills. John Hustle will always retain a certain pushiness of style, but his suits, shirts and ties are a now more decorous and suitable to the promotion which he thinks is his due. Alan Grey has splashed out and got a rather better-cut suit, has thrown away his 1960s ties, goes to the hairdresser once a month, and realises that he no longer has to live up to his name. He too can make a better personal impact on others. David Wright, who started out with a strong head-start over his two colleagues, is going to have to work even harder to keep ahead. He too has learnt a lot of home truths about his own personal grooming, his voice level, his pace of delivery, his eye contact. He will make it to the very top largely by having improved his personal projection performance.

What I have described above is, very simply, about improving your personal impact credit-rating by carefully reading the signs of how others read you. There may be some apparent gimmicks in the book, but this is not a gimmicky subject. We only have to remind ourselves, once again, how many causes have been lost, not because of the substance or the subject matter, but because of bad communication, bad presentation, and bad impacting which has destroyed the credibility that that subject deserved.

Most successful people spend time in personal coaching and training sessions. Books like this can never teach those skills but what they can do is provide some of the basic groundwork against which that learning can more easily take place. Personal impact matters. Remember those three candidates with identical CVs and work experience. The one who communicated best, won.

# APPENDIX

# Form Reports

> *All dress conventions can be made to seem as ridiculous as fig leaves. In the long eye of history, a necktie is a silly thing . . .*
>
> The Times

There is a story that the golf champion Jack Nicklaus goes to an old professional friend once a year and says: 'Teach me to play golf.' True or false, it is a useful illustration of the fact that people at the top of the tree, people who are constantly in the public eye, also need to go back to basics from time to time. In terms of the personal impact you make on others, as in all walks of life, you don't need to be ill to get better. To change the metaphor, even if you have got a superb hi-fi sound system, with the most up-to-date speakers and amplifiers and so on, if the stylus or pick-up heads are dirty, worn or defective, then the music will jar.

To illustrate some of the points made in this book, the following brief analyses of a few top people are offered in a spirit of constructive criticism. By the time the book reaches the shops some of my comments may be slightly out of date. I hope so. It may mean that those few unfortunates who are criticised in the form reports that follow, have realised how much personal impact matters. Several of them are included however, because, quite simply, they are among the best contemporary communicators, from whom we could all learn a great deal.

\* \* \*

*Name*:       John Major

*Occupation*:   Prime Minister

*Presence*:    Politically correct. A neat, perfectly well turned-out tailor dummy look. Not a hair out of place (is it gel-ed?). His large upper lip gives him an over-serious, little boy, 'earnest camel' appearance. But he also can project a straightforward, honest charm.

*Dress sense*:  Nothing to fault. It has got much better now that his tailors and clothiers have to come to him and have an interest in his wearing their better-looking products. His shirt collars still tend to be of a slightly too mean cut.

*Paralanguage*: As already discussed elsewhere in the book, his parenthetical style of speaking is better than his detractors give him credit for. He projects weakly and does not sound like a man with strong philosophical principles. His voice is reasonably pitched, but the emphasis and tone lack the gravitas and authority that his position demands.

*Content*:     He has a weak habit of repeating certain words, even important ones, twice in the same sentence. The mimics have warned him off some of his more tiresome repetitions. His content looks as it sounds, as if much of it has been prepared by his advisers and civil servants. It is cautious officialese.

*Conclusions*:     He does, whatever he may say, need more training in how to put across to his audience that he actually believes in what he preaches. He thinks that by merely raising his voice, he achieves this, but it does not work. It still sounds weak. He needs to use his charm much more directly, get better speech-writers, and inject even more drama into what he says, otherwise people will stop listening.

\* \* \*

*Name*:          John Smith

*Occupation*:    Leader of the Opposition

*Presence*:      Unprepossessing. He is not good at political theatre or the theatre of politics. According to some Labour Party critics he is slow and unspectacular in private as well. Ken Livingstone is, however, quoted as saying, 'There is the air of preying mantis about him. Or the hunting spider. He's no tortoise. He is quick witted. He just hides it very well.' As he speaks he swings his head and body like a metronome, left to right. He used always to speak with his arms down at his sides as if on parade. Now he does a bit of contrived fist-pounding, but it still looks artificial.

*Dress sense*:   Dull and conformist. But what most impresses first is the size of his spectacles. They even dwarf the large expanse of his bald forehead and his great chin, giving him a blinkered, myopic look, and, more than anything else, 'create' the bank clerk impression that the television-viewing public have of him.

*Paralanguage*: A great cliché monger. Flat and boring, though he has a pleasant enough voice in

private. There is no perceived drama in his
oratory which leads to the belief that he
(like the Prime Minister) has no strength of
feeling underlying what he says. He is
incapable of changing tone sufficiently
to match his audience, and is, consequently,
much better in small groups or in the
House of Commons where his acerbic
wit shows through. In front of great
gatherings he looks as if he is always
holding back from becoming too dramatic.

*Content*: Good and clear and cleverly strung together,
though see 'clichés' above.

*Conclusions*: Like the Prime Minister, he lacks what his
colleagues call 'the vision thing'. No amount
of training can produce charisma in an
uncharismatic personality, but there are
serious image improvements that could be
made. He must get a more fitting pair of
glasses, dare to smile a little, and let the real
wit that is there hang out much more. He
should go for less 'dumpy' suits, and he
should search out new speech-writers.

\* \* \*

*Name*:          Paddy Ashdown

*Occupation*:    Party Leader

*Presence*:      More impressive on the box than off it. He knows better than anyone else in politics how he looks and how he comes across on the small screen. He appears cool, calm and boyishly unfluttered. There is a slightly anxious air about him sometimes; his brows knit, as if slightly puzzled, helped by what looks like a dramatic old scar across his forehead. He slits his eyes like the soldier he once was, as if against the storm of tough questioning. But he has good eyelock. He uses his hands powerfully to emphasise key points.

*Dress sense*:   Good at choosing shirts, ties and suits, but he obviously takes greater care (naturally) when he is going to be interviewed. In real life he can be less prepossessing.

*Paralanguage*:  Like his predecessors David Owen and David Steel (and why are they all so good at presenting and yet fail to pick up votes?) he is particularly effective in his use of voice-tone, pitch and timing. He is perceived to believe in what he is saying and will not be browbeaten by interviewers.

*Conclusions*: One of the best performers on British television. Could try to be a bit less serious and worried looking.

\* \* \*

| | |
|---|---|
| *Name*: | Lord (David) Owen |
| *Occupation*: | International statesman |
| *Presence*: | His much-discussed satanic good looks are matched by a clear and dedicated mind. He suffers fools badly, which is no bad thing except that in his case, along with his very short attention span (or boredom threshold), it shows up all too clearly. His laidback, apparent arrogance, may, according to friends, cloak a shyness, but that is far from apparent, as he appears to have lost all modesty long ago. |
| *Dress sense*: | Understated. In detail, uncaring. |
| *Paralanguage*: | He has a sort of languorous drawl in his speech-pattern which can appear casual even though his actual words are ruthless, harsh and very much to the point. |

*Content*:        He knows exactly what he wants to say and says it. There is little fat or padding.

*Conclusions*:    He is almost certainly too set in his ways to change.

*   *   *

*Name*:           John Harvey-Jones

*Occupation*:     Business leader and media personality

*Presence*:       With his long hair and moustache of a different shade, Mr Harvey-Jones is, like Richard Branson, an unlikely looking industrialist. (Military-style moustaches in older men usually go with short back and sides hair-cuts.) But his brisk, flamboyant approach to life – even at seventy and following a most successful business career – has given him a perceived character that has made him one of the most unexpected and popular new figures in British television, with his *Troubleshooter* series. This is in stark contrast to the hard-man image which he had when he was the ruthless boss of ICI. Now, as he says, he is a business agony aunt.

*Dress sense*: Contrived style; expansive; very colourful ties and jaunty breast-pocket handkerchiefs. These are deliberately chosen to accentuate his already colourful character. It all makes for a highly recognisable package.

*Paralanguage*: His non-stop commentaries on business life are part and parcel of a very personal image. He is not a great orator but his wit, sharpness, and brisk, no-nonsense approach, make him a popular public speaker. People listen because they know he will be both amusing and informative.

*Content*: He lards his words, deliberately, with lots of rank-and-file expletives. 'Bloody' is one of his most common adjectives, and that too is, deliberate or not, part of his down-to-earth, man-of-the-people act. Being left of centre politically has also marked him out.

*Conclusions*: Like Branson, he is a man who has moulded his own particular public persona. Not someone one would wish to change. He is what he is, and as a communicator he is one of the best.

\* \* \*

*Name*:          Hillary Clinton

*Occupation*:    First Lady

*Presence*:      I have chosen a transatlantic example because Mrs Clinton's recent image-change has been much written about since her husband stepped into the political ring. She starts with one great advantage: she looks much tougher, more sharp and intelligent, and less pleased with herself than her husband. Moving on from Pat Buchanan's description of her as 'a lawyer's spouse', she has come, seen and largely conquered. And she has buried the 'pain' that her husband has caused her. She has moved from dowdyish provincialism, long, unkempt, hippie hair and big glasses, to up-market charm-school product in a very short period of time. She benefits from innate good looks, good cheekbones, good confidence. She has taken to contact lenses and lost a stone in weight.

*Dress sense*:   It wasn't there – and simply wasn't bothered about or considered important enough before – 'I thought make-up was superficial and silly' – but it certainly is now. Dress sense at the top is largely (particularly in terms of women) a factor of their fashion advisers, and she/they are winning over the most recent examples of First Lady dressing styles. It's helped by her lack of vanity, which has class. Early on in the Presidential campaign, she got to grips with her looks, hair and clothes, and, gently and subtly, she changed.

*Paralanguage*: Yet to be fully developed. But she is competent without being glib.

*Content*: She has already had lessons in image and impact and in the use of the sound-bite. She'll end up better than the President.

*Conclusions*: She's good in a fix as her outburst over his rumoured infidelities showed: 'I'm sittin' here because I love him, and I honour what he's been through, and what we've been through together, and you know, if that's not enough for people, then, heck, don't vote for him.' It stopped the rot of scandal in a way that others on this side of the Atlantic could learn from. There is little image crimpers can teach her about tactics or personal impact skills now. She is, in the words of the *Washington Post*, 'loaded with symbolic cargo'. And she has a back-up team that will make it work. She is becoming the almost perfect role model. Her husband never will be.

*Name:*            George Carey

*Occupation:*      Archbishop of Canterbury

*Presence:*        Presence is enormously important in a
                   churchman or woman. In contemporary
                   times when faith is weak, churches, if they
                   are to survive, need strong, confident
                   leaders, and to be seen to be resolute in their
                   beliefs. Tradition of dress and language is
                   cast aside only at great risk. Sadly, the
                   present incumbent does not inspire by any
                   of these things. He is a pleasant enough
                   man, but distinction, gravitas and the other
                   intangibles of presence are distinctly lacking.
                   It is not his fault, but the big gap between
                   his front teeth which shows in close-up is a
                   serious distraction.

*Dress sense:*     It has to be a personal opinion, but for one
                   not of his church, his less traditional,
                   rainbow style vestments do not work. They
                   are pantomime rather than dramatic theatre
                   and it would need a more charismatic leader
                   than him to be able to wear them with the
                   authority that is required. His new dress
                   code is not liberalism, but merely drawing
                   the line of convention at a different place.
                   Dress codes can easily be mocked, but they

can destroy much more than the fabric of
their cloth.

*Paralanguage*: It is just passable in a churchy sort of way,
but the tone and drama are absent.

*Content*: No comment.

*Conclusions*: Without demanding fire or passion,
blandness should at least be kept to a
minimum. The Church of England has, for
its reasons, chosen its leader. To many inside
and outside that body it has sacrificed
serious impact on the altar of trying to be
modern. The Archbishop's impact is the less
because the man, an honourable and
well-meaning figure, carries little weight,
has a very slight recognition factor, and
projects no drama whatsoever.

\* \* \*

*Name*: Madonna

*Occupation*: Mega pop star

*Presence*: Strikingly unignorable both on and off stage.
Too much has been written about her
on-stage presence. Let me concentrate on

what (limited) experience I have of her off-stage impact. It is claimed that she once said 'losing my virginity was a career move,' and everything about her seems to live up to this desire to shock. But from her television interviews something more surprising shows through: behind the mega-hype there is a highly intelligent woman waiting to get out. She has style.

*Dress sense*: Constantly changing, ranging from the conventional to the shockingly provocative. Each new project ushers in a new image. She can be a sophisticate – a latter-day Garbo or Dietrich – or an innocent, as in the baby-doll nightdress shots taken for *Vanity Fair*. Highly stylised. Odd but very effective.

*Paralanguage*: Her delivery style belies her stage extravagances. She is distinctly subdued, but enunciates clearly and well. She looks as if she could subdue anyone if riled or angered.

*Content*: Very thoughtful and deliberate. In contrast to most politicians, she appears to write all her own lines and think all her own thoughts. She learnt early on how the fame system operates and very adroitly exploited it. She knows exactly what to say to provoke a response.

*Conclusions*:  President Mitterrand said of Margaret Thatcher that she had the eyes of Caligula and the lips of Marilyn Monroe. There is something similar about Madonna. Tough, brazen, icy, subtle. Everything she does is totally, absolutely deliberate. She knows *exactly* the effect she is having, *all the time*. In that, she is a rare species.

* * *

*Name*:  Clive James

*Occupation*:  Professional Australian, wit, author and television personality.

*Presence*:  Early on in his television career his unconventional image was off-putting to some viewers, but as he has matured, he has won  his critics over and created an image that is  entirely his own. Content always takes priority over style, although recently he has swopped his casual dress for more well-cut suits.

*Dress sense*:  For him almost any move would have to be up the sartorial tree. His (deliberately) slobby style, his lack of disguising his girth, has turned from a PR nightmare into an effective professional quirk or gimmick.

*Paralanguage*: A very clever man. His delivery, like his writing, flows endlessly and is conspicuously undramatic, needing, at its best, a lot of very attentive listening, but making his point very cleverly in the end.

*Content*: There is no doubt that his content is his own. He has a whimsical style of speaking (and writing) that is uniquely Clive James. He also has that great ability to commentate imaginatively on major events and personalities, as in his series 'Fame in the Twentieth Century', but at the same time to keep an excellent sense of humour that pricks pomposity and cuts bigots to size.

*Conclusions*: He has an agreeable charm about him which belies the other impression of being a bit of an old bruiser.

\* \* \*

*Name*: Richard Branson

*Occupation*: Business entrepreneur

*Presence*: 'If Branson had worn a pair of steel-rimmed glasses, a double-breasted suit and shaved off his beard, we would have taken him seriously'. So said a senior British Airways executive after the airline had to pay Branson exemplary damages over their dirty tricks campaign. This again underlines the importance of image in the eyes of rivals as well as colleagues, and how deceptive it can be. I have to admit that if I had been called in to advise Branson on his personal image, I would probably have suggested changes on the above lines. Branson has prospered despite his image. But his tactics are always quick and sure-footed, and you have to be a Branson to get away with it.

*Dress sense*: As discussed above. He claims he has not bought clothes in twenty years; his wife buys them all. It shows. Casualness is all. Normally only Israeli cabinet ministers can get away with not wearing ties. But then most successful entrepreneurs do not travel the Atlantic by balloon or on their own airline fleet.

*Paralanguage*:  Richard Branson's language and paralanguage are, on first meeting him, remarkably unstructured, even confused. He does not express himself particularly well, and his voice tones and stress patterns are flat. But the gleam in the eye, the belief in what he is saying, carries him through.

*Content*:  Good, especially with smaller groups.

*Conclusions*:  He is someone who has succeeded and will probably continue to do so without worrying at all about his personal image (in contrast with his concern for the image of Virgin and his other business activities). He is a difficult role model for anyone to emulate. The top echelons of business life are not filled with such examples. It is difficult to make many recommendations, but on my experience of him, he could do even better by learning to marshall his arguments and improve his delivery when he is speaking to groups of strangers for the first time.

*   *   *

| | |
|---|---|
| *Name*: | Glenda Jackson |
| *Occupation*: | Actress and Member of Parliament |
| *Presence*: | Her selection as a Labour Member of Parliament for Hampstead and Highgate provoked a great deal of derisory comment, though why an actress should be less acceptable as a politician than, say, a lawyer, is not clear. After all, Ronald Reagan played his part as President quite well, and politics and acting, or, more precisely, histrionics, have very much in common. For both you need to know how to contrive sincerity, passion and belief, to convince your audience. Glenda Jackson has that but in her Parliamentary performances she seems to hold back and be deliberately moderate and understated. |
| *Dress sense*: | For someone who played the magnificently dressed Queen Elizabeth I, her standard dress sense is far from inspiring, and tends to the Fabian-Oxfam mode. Because of who she is she gets away with sometimes looking like a own-market Shirley Williams. |
| *Paralanguage*: | She is, unlike many actors and actresses, less addicted to a 'stagey' way of speaking of the 'luvvies' variety. Her voice is her own and it |

has a style and pitch that makes her very
listenable to.

*Content*: No comment.

*Conclusions*: Glenda Jackson is what she is. People perceive her in terms of parts she has played in the past. She is yet to hold attention in her new role and will only do so if she develops an impact in that role that matches her talents.

\* \* \*

*Name*: Jeremy Paxman

*Occupation*: Television pundit or hitman

*Presence*: Cynicism personified. He looks as if he is always on the point of yawning as he awaits answers to his questions. Cabinet Ministers are said to fear this latter-day Robin Day. But he knows that it is the hinge that squeaks with the right kind of sound that gets the grease. His brilliance shows through the bumptiousness. He is a man who appears to have lost his modesty at a distinctly early age, as befits someone who graduated via Esther Rantzen's 'That's Life' programme.

*Dress sense*: A touch of the effortlessly superior. He knows what he's wearing and what effect it has on others.

*Paralanguage*: His supercilious, arrogant, almost facetious style of commentary can infuriate or fascinate, but is difficult to ignore. His tone exemplifies the 'come off it', anti-deferential school of interviewing.

*Content*: He is a clever operator. Even the apparent lack of precision in some of his questions is probably deliberate. He knows precisely what he wants to get out of an interview, and can reduce opponents to a level of 'look what the cat's brought in.'

*Conclusions*: He is someone who had deliberately established his public personality. You either like it or hate it, but one way or the other, he is not going to change.

\* \* \*

How do you yourself match up? Try seeing how you appear to others. Few of us are good at the self-realisation game but there is no down-side in making the attempt.

*Name*:

*Occupation*:

*Presence*:

*Dress sense*:

*Paralanguage*:

*Content*:

*Conclusions*: